ESSENTIAL MENORCA

TRIANGLE BOOKS

CONTENTS

MENORCA: SOME ESSENTIAL FACTS 4

TEN ESSENTIAL PLACES 6

TEN ESSENTIAL EXPERIENCES 14

HISTORY TIMELINE 22

EXPLORING MENORCA'S VILLAGES 24

WINDMILLS 30

BRITISH MENORCA 36

THE FORTRESS TRAIL 62

TRADITIONAL MENORCA 82

HEAVEN ON EARTH 84

ISLANDS WITHIN AN ISLAND 90

LIGHTHOUSES 98

THE BEST SUNSETS 126

EXPLORING MENORCA'S GREEN LANDSCAPE 136

A JOURNEY TO THE PAST 144

THE CAMÍ DE CAVALLS 148

SIGHTSEEING BY BIKE AND ATB 150

MADE IN MENORCA 152

MENORCA: SOME ESSENTIAL FACTS

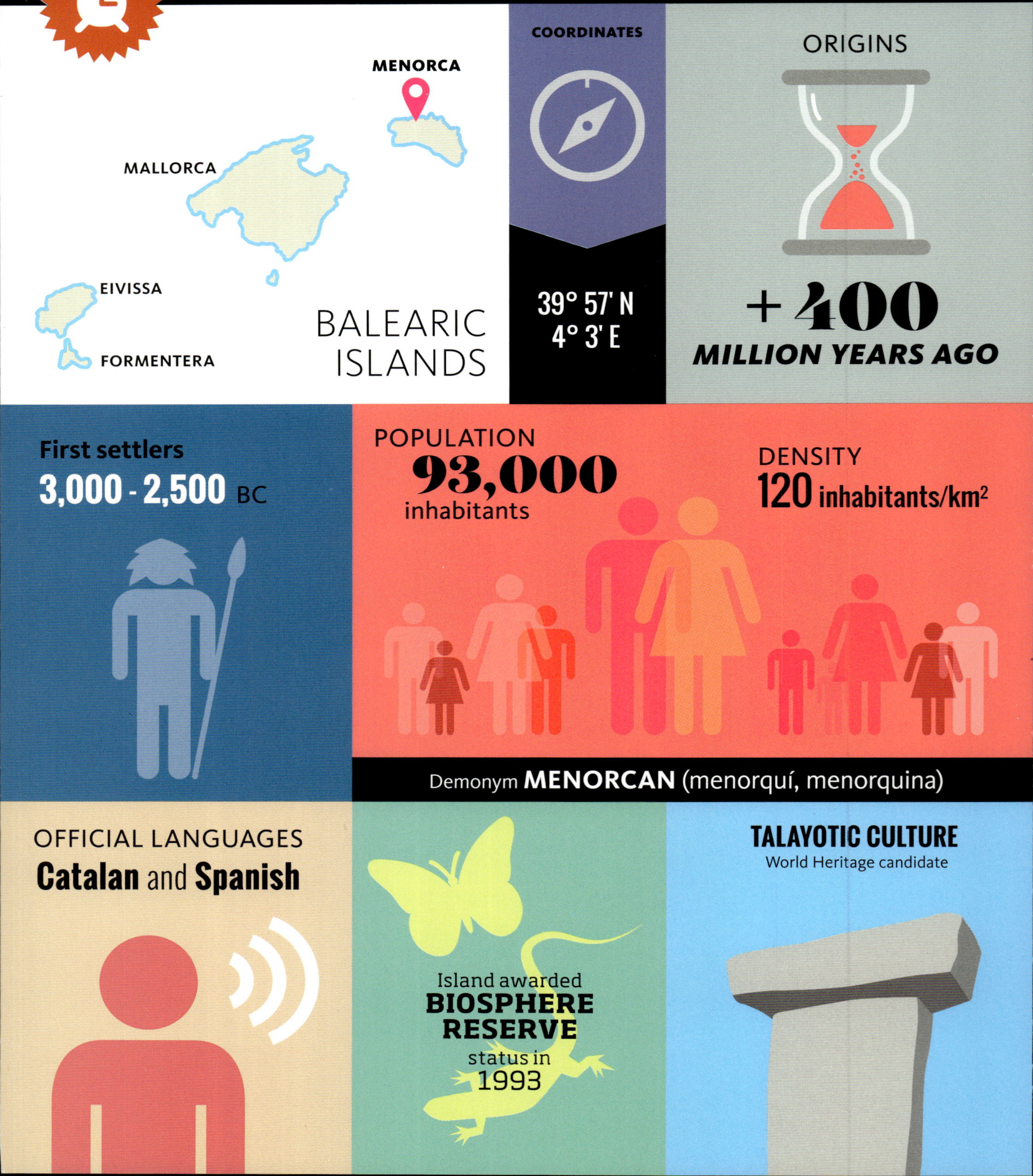

SURFACE AREA
702 km²

66 %
PROTECTED SURFACE AREA

5,7 %
BUILT AREA

216 km
COASTLINE

More than
100
COVES and **BEACHES**

Maximum altitude
EL TORO
(358 m)

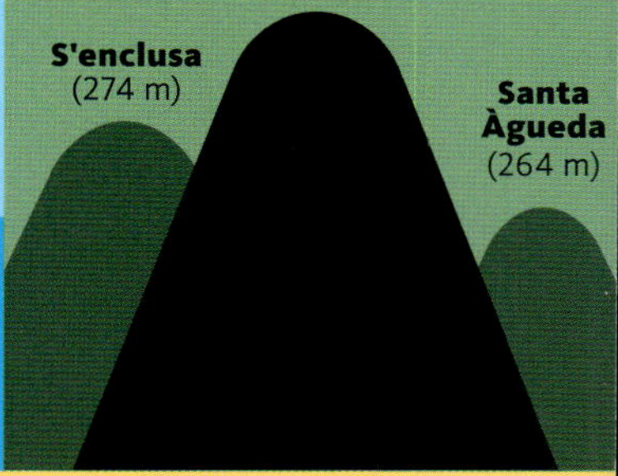

SEVEN LIGHTHOUSES

ADMINISTRATIVE STRUCTURE
8 municipalities

Camí de cavalls

A **184-km-long** bridle path that encircles the island

MEDITERRANEAN CLIMATE

Hours of daylight
+2,500
hours/year

16-18°C
Average temperature

Average rainfall
540 mm/year

The island's essential places include natural sites, unique landmarks, cultural attractions, beauty spots and other places that encapsulate and epitomise the essence of this Mediterranean island.

TEN ESSENTIAL **PLACES**

Favàritx

S'Albufera des Grau

Menorca Cathedral

Museu de Menorca

Maó harbour

El Toro

Binibèquer Vell

Naveta des Tudons

Calesfonts

Pedreres de s'Hostal

1

Favàritx

The geological features on this section of the Maó coast make it one of the most unique places on the island. In addition to ancient rocky outcrops, you'll find sites of breathtaking beauty. Favàritx lies within the Albufera des Grau Natural Park, one of Menorca's most beautiful natural areas, which offers a wealth of flora and fauna.

► p. 98

2

The Albufera des Grau Natural Park

Road from Maó to Es Grau, 3.5 km marker post

The Albufera des Grau Natural Park lies in the centre of the Biosphere Reserve. Covering 5,067 ha it is home to the island's largest wetland area.

▸ p. **136**

3

Menorca Cathedral

Cal Bisbe, 8 (Ciutadella)

This is the island's main place of worship. Built between the 13th and 14th centuries on the site of the grand mosque in the former Medina, it was restored in the 16th and 19th centuries. The neoclassical door on the main façade covers the original Gothic one.

4

Museu de Menorca

Av. Doctor Guàrdia, s/n (Maó)

The island's museum, the Museu de Menorca, is housed in the former Franciscan convent in Maó. Its collections include highly valuable archaeological relics and works of art from different civilisations and periods in history. An essential cultural attraction.

5

Maó harbour

Stretching for over 5 km, Maó harbour is the largest natural harbour in Europe and the second largest in the world, after Pearl Harbour. It is well worth a visit.

► p. **46**

6

El Toro

Standing 358 metres above sea level, this is the highest mountain on the island. The panoramic views make it worthy of the title 'essential'. We recommend a climb to the top on a clear day.

► p. **57**

7

Binibèquer Vell

Sant Lluís

With its whitewashed houses, Binibèquer Vell in many ways resembles a village on the Greek islands and exudes the purest essence of the Mediterranean. You'll find some interesting facts about it in the chapter "Exploring Menorca's villages".

▸ p. **29**

8

Naveta des Tudons

Me-1 road, 40 km marker post (Ciutadella)

Its excellent state of repair and unique shape make this the most iconic monument from the talayotic culture. The remains of more than 100 individuals were found inside.

▸ p. **144**

9

Calesfonts

Es Castell

This cove in Maó harbour is very popular with tourists and has all the ingredients to keep visitors of all ages and backgrounds entertained: the distinctive skyline, the fishing village atmosphere, the pavement cafés along the seafront and a great choice of food. Who would deny its 'essential' status?

▸ p. **34**

10

Pedreres de s'Hostal

Camí Vell de Maó, km 1 (Ciutadella)

The ancient quarries, Pedreres de s'Hostal, were restored in the middle of the 1990s and have become a unique cultural visitor attraction on Menorca. We recommend you explore this vast sandstone labyrinth.

We often make the mistake of visiting a destination without really experiencing it. The fact is, photos can't replace experiences. Below you'll find some essential activities to give you a complete overview of Menorca.

TEN ESSENTIAL **EXPERIENCES**

Go kayaking
Explore the Camí de Cavalls
Sample Menorcan cuisine
Travel back in time
Admire a cultural gem
Experience Menorca's festivals
Shop at fairs and markets
Visit a winery and cheese makers
Discover the underwater world
Enjoy a sunset

1

Go kayaking

Is it safe to say that Menorca is one of the best places in the world to go kayaking? We certainly think so. Whether you go along the north or south coast, kayaking trips are always memorable

2

Explore the Camí de Cavalls

Divided into 20 stages and stretching for 184 km, the ancient bridle path, the Camí de Cavalls, is, arguably, the best place to discover the island from the inside. If you want to know the best sections to explore, take a look at the chapter "Exploring Menorca's green landscape".

► pp. **148-149**

3

Sample Menorcan cuisine

As the saying goes: "When in Rome, do as the Romans do". One of the best ways of getting to know a destination is through its food. So, if you're travelling to Menorca, skip the international cuisine and sample some local dishes.

► p. **156**

4

Travel back in time

Some people say that Menorca is an open-air museum. And with good reason. The island has more than 1,500 archaeological sites, a high density for an island covering just 702 km^2: that's two per km^2. We'll tell you about them in the chapter "A journey to the past".

► p. **144**

5

Admire a cultural gem

Costa d'en Deià, 40 (Maó)

Going to a concert, play or bel canto recital at Spain's oldest opera house is one of the cultural experiences you can't afford to miss if you come to Menorca. Put the Teatre Principal in Maó on your itinerary.

► p. **42**

6

Experience Menorca's festivals

Ciutadella

The festivals of Sant Joan, in Ciutadella, are the best-known ones on the island and attract the largest crowds. But they're not the only ones. Throughout the summer, all the towns and villages on the island celebrate their festivals dedicated to their respective patron saints, with horses as their centrepiece. We invite you to discover them.

► pp. **82-83**

7

Shop at fairs and markets

In addition to the fish market, the Mercat des Peix, in Ciutadella, and Sa Plaça and Sa Peixateria in Maó, Menorca has a vast array of fairs and markets. You'll find them selling farm produce, handicrafts, specific and general-purpose goods, during the day, in the evening and late at night, in towns and villages across the island... In summer, every day is market day on the island.

8

Visit a winery and cheese makers

Wine and cheese are two of the most famous products Made in Menorca. This means that a tour of a winery and cheese makers are two essential experiences. For further details, see the chapter "Made in Menorca".

► p. **153**

9

Discover the underwater world

The quality of Menorca's waters makes it a unique place for snorkelling and scuba diving. Best of all is the presence of shipwrecked vessels along the coast which contribute to the wealth of marine flora and fauna.

10

Enjoy a sunset

Sunsets are one of the great spectacles of nature. You can catch them all over the island and experience a magical dusk. Take a look at our selection.

► p. 126

HISTORY TIMELINE

Menorca's position in the western Mediterranean, almost equidistant from the Iberian Peninsula and Sardinia, the Languedoc region and Algeria, has made it a much-coveted place throughout the centuries. The easternmost of the Balearic Islands is an extraordinarily rich treasure trove of historic episodes.

2,500 BC
The first settlers arrive.

1,500-123 BC
Talayotic era.

123 BC
Roman conquest of Menorca by the consul Quintus Caecilius Metellus.

73 AD
Iamo (Ciutadella) and Mago (Maó) are proclaimed Roman municipalities.

5th century
Establishment of Christianity on Menorca.

903
Muslim conquest of Menorca.

1232-1287
Menorca agrees to come under the rule of the Crown of Aragon and remains the only Muslim redoubt in the Balearic Islands.

1287
Christian conquest by the king of the Crown of Aragon, Alfonso III.

1348
The population declines due to the Black Death pandemic.

1535 and 1558
Turkish raids on Maó and Ciutadella.

16th-17th centuries
A tumultuous time. Menorca builds its defence structures: the castles of Sant Felip and Sant Antoni and the new walls around Ciutadella.

1708-1756
First period of British rule. The Treaty of Utrecht (1713) recognised English sovereignty over the island.

1756-1763
Menorca comes under French rule.

1763-1782
Second period of British rule.

1782-1798
Spain gains control of Menorca.

1798-1802
Third period of British rule.

1802
Menorca returns permanently to Spanish rule with the signing of the Treaty of Amiens.

1830
Large-scale migration of islanders to Algeria.

1850-1900
Industrialisation of the island: founding of the factories La Industrial Mahonesa and Societat del Vapor Maonès.

1906
"L'any de sa fam" (the year of the hunger). The industrial crisis on Menorca leads to mass emigration to Cuba, Argentina and Uruguay.

1936-1939
Menorca aligns itself with the government of the Republic during the Spanish Civil War and its population suffers harsh reprisals.

1939-1975
Franco's dictatorship. People's rights and freedoms are revoked and Menorca's language and culture are relegated to the domestic sphere.

1975-1978
Spanish transition to democracy.

1978
The Spanish Constitution is approved.

1979
The island's government, the Consell Insular de Menorca, is established. Menorca spearheads calls to introduce government bodies to the other Balearic islands.

1983
The Balearic Islands approve their Autonomy Statute which establishes the names and territorial boundaries of the community, its self-ruling bodies, powers and official languages. The statute was revised and a new one approved in 2007.

1993
Menorca named a Biosphere Reserve by UNESCO.

EXPLORING MENORCA'S VILLAGES

MENORCA is divided into eight administrative municipalities, to which we must also add the towns of Fornells and Sant Climent. The last census of the island places its population at 93,000 inhabitants, with two thirds of these living, in equal parts, in Maó and Ciutadella.

It could, therefore, be said that the island of Menorca has two centres of gravity and a two-pronged population structure. Do you want to find out a little more about this island and discover the secrets of its towns and villages? Here are some of the most important ones.

SANT LLUÍS

The typical dazzling white hues of the island are shown at their best in this small town on the southern coast. Harmony and balance define the architecture and layout of the only town on Menorca to be founded by the French.

SANT LLUÍS

Founded
1761 **(separated from Maó in 1904)**

Population
7,500 approx.

Surface area
34.7 km²

Density
215 inhabitants/km²

Traditional villages
Es Consell
Es Pou Nou
Torret
S'Ullastrar
Binifadet

Residential developments
S'Algar
Alcalfar
Punta Prima
Biniancolla
Cala Torret
Binibèquer
Binissafúller
Cap d'en Font

Sant Lluís beaches
Cala de Biniparratx
Es Caló Blanc
Cala de Binissafúller
Es Caló Fondo
Cala de Binibèquer
Cala Torret
Cala de Biniancolla
Platja de Punta Prima
Caló Roig
Cala d'Alcalfar
Caló d'en Rafalet

www.ajsantlluis.org

Es Molí de Dalt

Standing at the entrance to Sant Lluís, this flour mill dating from the middle of the 18th century, has become the town's iconic landmark. It houses the ethnology museum, the Museu Etnològic Municipal.

▸ p. 30

← Church of Sant Lluís and Pla de sa Creu

The first building in the town of Sant Lluís, this late 18th-century church is a clear example of the prevailing neo-classical trends of the time. The church stands in the Pla de Sa Creu, in front of the town hall. In the middle of the square stands an obelisk placed there on the orders of the governor of Menorca, the Comte de Lannion, in honour of Louis XV, the king of France when the town was founded.

The *joc de sa bolla*

This game, which is similar to pétanque, was introduced to Menorca under French rule (1756-1763). There is currently only one *jugadero*, or *joc de la bolla* court, in Sant Lluís. In the photo, Elias Cardona, the most senior player of this unique sport (he started playing at the age of 7).

The *caseríos*

It is well worth taking a break to explore on foot, or by bike, the farmsteads, or *caseríos*, in Sant Lluís. Es Pou Nou, Es Consell, Torret and S'Ullastrar retain the defining elements of rural Menorcan architecture: drystone walls, typical whitewashed houses, wild olive wood fences... Tradition, authenticity and a haven of peace.

TOP 10 PLACES

Binibèquer Vell

This small tourist resort in Sant Lluís is one of the island's most charming spots. Completely whitewashed and with forms and contours similar to villages on the Greek islands, Binibèquer Vell is viewed as an example of the Mediterranean essence at its purest. It was built between 1964 and 1968, to a project carried out by Javier Barba Corsini and Antonio Sintes.

Wine production

Binifadet was one of the first wineries to produce wine with the **Vi de la Terra Illa de Menorca** Designation of Origin. Over the years, it has established a reputation as one of the island's top wine producers. Binifadet runs guided tours of its facilities and vineyards, and also holds wine tastings. It has a bar and restaurant.

WINDMILLS

There are 30 surviving windmills, watermills, fire-powered and animal-powered mills. Many of them lie in ruins, and initiatives have been launched to recover this valuable ethnological heritage. Some of the most important flour mills are the **Molí de Dalt** and the **Molí de Baix** in Sant Lluís, the first is home to the Museu Etnològic Municipal; the **Molí Vell** the **Molí de la Santa Creu**, standing at the entrance to Es Castell; the **Molí des Racó** in Es Mercadal; and the **Molí des Comte** in Ciutadella, both with a restaurant.

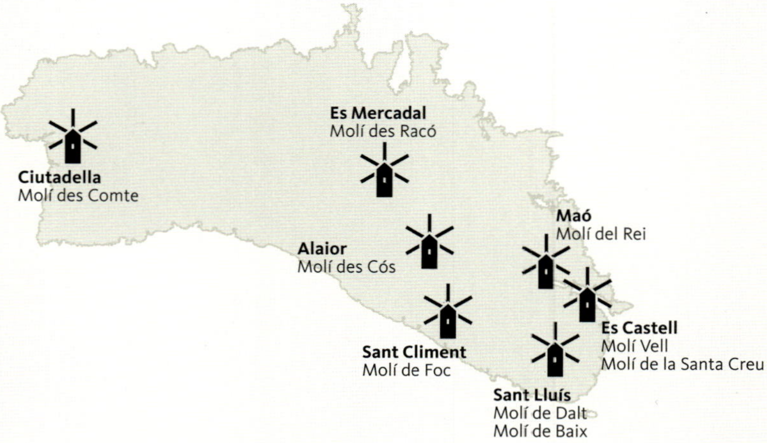

Molí Vell, in Es Castell.

Molí des Racó, in Es Mercadal.

Molí de Dalt, in Sant Lluís.

The Molí de Dalt is home to the **Museu Etnològic Municipal**. Utensils and tools take us back to ancient rural life and traditional crafts.

ES CASTELL

Founded by the British in the 18th century who named it Georgetown. Following the Spanish conquest, it was renamed Real Villa de San Carlos, which was shortened to Villacarlos. In 1985, it was renamed Es Castell.

ES CASTELL

Founded
18th century

Population
8,000 approx.

Surface area
11.6 km^2

Density
215 inhabitants/km^2

Residential developments
El Fonduco
Son Vilar
Santa Anna
Sol del Este
Cala Sant Esteve
Trebalúger

www.aj-escastell.org

The first rays of sunshine

Menorca is the most easterly part of Spain and Es Castell is the easternmost municipality on Menorca. This means that its inhabitants are the first in the country to see the sun rise every day. The installation, *The Gateway of Eos*, by the artist Francesc Calvet, pays tribute to the Greek goddess of the dawn and is the best place to see daybreak.

S'Esplanada

The former parade ground forms the core of the urban layout of Es Castell. The plaza is set between three military buildings: the Conde de Cifuentes, Duque de Crillón and Cala Corb barracks (the latter is now home to the military museum, the Museu Militar de Menorca). The town hall stands on one side, surmounted by a clock tower and belfry. If you want to know more about British architecture, look at the chapter "British Menorca".

► p. 36

TOP 10 PLACES

Calesfonts

This cove in Maó harbour is a favourite with tourists and has all the ingredients to keep visitors of all ages and backgrounds entertained: the charming skyline which belies the British influence, the fishing village atmosphere, the pavement cafés along the seafront, a great choice of food and the nightlife. Who would deny its 'essential' status? Well, certainly not us. Here's a tip: it is well worth walking to the peaceful wharf, the Moll d'en Pons, and enjoying the full moon in the summer months.

Cala Sant Esteve

This tiny cove on the coast features some of the most iconic buildings from Menorca's military past: Fort Marlborough, the castle of Sant Felip, and the Stuart Tower. It is certainly one of the parts of the island most steeped in history. In the section "The fortress trail" you'll find a few insights into its heritage.

▸ p. **62**

Llaüt

The *llaüt* is a typical Menorcan boat. Originally, the *mestres d'aixa* (master carpenters of the shore) built them by hand from locally sourced wood.

Church of El Roser

The church in Es Castell was built at the end of the 18th and beginning of the 19th centuries in the neo-classical style. The baptismal font and stone altarpiece inside are from the old chapel of the castle of Sant Felip.

BRITISH MENORCA

Menorca was ruled by the British crown from 1708 and 1802, a tumultuous decade which included two brief periods of French and Spanish rule (see **History timeline**, pp. 22-23). The British influence still endures today in its military buildings, civil architecture, town planning, language and customs. Below you will find some of the most important architects and landmarks.

Mackellar's urban planning

Es Castell is a fine example of the application of the principles of British military urban planning, with the parade ground, S'Esplanada, as its centrepiece. The town was designed by Scottish engineer Patrick Mackellar.

Richard Kane

Richard Kane (1662-1736) was appointed British crown governor of Menorca in 1716. He was responsible for building the path, the Camí d'en Kane, and the rainwater-collection and storage tank, the *aljub* in Es Mercadal. He is buried at the castle of Sant Felip, the fortress extended while he was governor.

Hospital of the Illa del Rei

Maó harbour

The military hospital built by the British was operational from the 18th century until the 1960s. The U-shaped building occupies a large area of the island. The chapel built by the Spanish in 1784 survives intact.

Camí d'en Kane

Today, the Camí d'en Kane is a peaceful byway set among beautiful scenery, but in the 18th century it was Menorca's main road. It was built on the orders of the governor Richard Kane – an obelisk at the beginning of the road to Fornells commemorates the fact – to make it easier to transport troops and artillery between Maó and Ciutadella which stand on opposite ends of the island.

The *aljub*

Es Mercadal

The *aljub*, or water-collection tank, in Es Mercadal, is another example of British civil architecture on the island. It was built in 1735 on the orders of the British governor Richard Kane to provide water for the troops crossing the island.

Illa Pinto

Maó harbour

The British built the naval base, Illa Pinto, in Maó harbour at the beginning of the 18th century. It is the only artificial island in the harbour and the site of a number of military buildings.

Son Granot and Hotel El Almirante

The municipality of Es Castell has two of the most remarkable examples of 18th-century civil architecture: the Son Granot and El Almirante hotels. Both buildings clearly show the influence of the classical-Palladian style the British brought to the island. Other fine examples are the Sant Antoni estate, in Maó harbour, and Son Bonaventura, in Alaior.

British vocabulary

The British legacy is not only found in the island's architecture. The Menorcan language has retained some interesting Anglicisms such as, for instance, **boínder** (bow window), **grevi** (gravy), **pinxa** (pilchard), **xoc** (chalk) and **ull blec** (black eye). Another example of the British influence is the **Dia d'Enganar** (April Fool's Day).

MAÓ

Maó is inextricably linked to its British past. It is, perhaps, together with Es Castell, the municipality that was most marked by the events of the 18th century. During this period of economic and cultural development it assumed the role of capital city and is still the main city on the island. Let's begin our route.

MAÓ

Founded
3rd century BC

Population
30,000 approx.

Surface area
117.2 km^2

Density
256 inhabitants/km^2

Residential developments
Sa Mesquida
Es Grau
Es Murtar
Sant Antoni
Cala Llonga
Canutells
Binidalí

Maó beaches
Cala Mesquida
Es Grau
Cala des Tamarells
Arenal de Morella
Arenal de Capifort
S'Enclusa
S'Arenalet de Mongofre

www.ajmao.org
www.mahon.es

The village of Sant Climent belongs to the municipality of Maó.

0
0,5
100 m
N
PORT DE MAÓ
PLA DE BAIXAMAR
PLA DES MONESTIR
S'HORT NOU
Costa de la Miranda
Sant Sebastià
Santa Teresa
Sant Elies
Plana
Santa Anna
Concepció
Plaça del Trianon
Carme
Camí des Castell
Plaça de la Miranda
Comerç
Can Victori
Claustre del Carme
Mercat de Maó
Plaça del Princep
E Carme
Moll de Llevant
San Fernando
Plaça del Carme
Costa de ses Voltes
Nord
Anuncivay
Ses Bruixes
Sa Peixateria
Arravaleta
Ca n'Oliver
Plaça Espanya
Infanta
Moll de Ponent
Biblioteca
Portal de Mar
Plaça de la Conquesta
Nou
Deià
Convent de la Concepció
Santa María
Àngel
Plaça Constitució
Parc des Freginal
Ajuntament
Principal de Guàrdia
Costa des General
Bon Aire
Sant Roc
Església
Alba
Hannover (Costa de sa Plaça)
Alaior
Bastió
Sant Jordi
Rector Mort
Isabel II
Plaça del Bastió
Sant Albert
Cós de Gràcia
Moll de Ponent
Portal de Sant Roc
Costa des Muret
sa Lluna
Sant Antoni
Sant Antoni
Dr. Orfila (ses Moreres)
Sant Josep
Sant Jeroni
Sant Jaume
Prieto i Caules (Arraval)
Forn
Sant Bartomeu
Sant Francesc
Frares
Negres
Ramis (Rovellada de Baix)
Comte Cifuentes (Rovellada de Dalt)
Pau
del Sol (la Clota)
Plaça de s'Esplanada
Museu de Menorca

Plaça de la Conquesta

This central square stands in the oldest part of the city on the site of the walled precincts of the medieval castle. It was laid out in the 1940s following the demolition of a group of houses behind the church of Santa Maria. On the northern side stands the Casa Mercadal (1761), currently home to the Mahon Public Library and History Archive. The statue is of the king of Aragon, Alfonso III.

Church of Santa Maria

Pl. Constitució, s/n

The building we see today dates from the late 18th century and stands on the foundations of the church King Alfonso III had built in 1288. Austere and solid in appearance on the outside, the interior houses two great treasures: the great organ with four keyboards and 3,006 pipes designed by Johan Kyburz and Francisco Otter, and the floor of the main nave, tiled in a pattern reminiscent of the tessellations of the mathematician Roger Penrose.

Portal de Sant Roc

This is the only surviving gate from the medieval city walls. It was built in the 14th century and marked the entrance to the Ciutadella road. It has been restored several times, the last one in the late 20th century.

Viewing point trail

This trail takes in the six viewing points in the centre of the town which boast complete panoramic views of Maó harbour. They are the Mirador de Sant Francesc, next to the church of Sant Francesc; the Pont des General, the starting point for the Costa des General and Costa des Muret, which connect the town centre and the harbour; the Mirador de Ses Monges, which was restored after being boarded up in the late 18th century; the Pont des Castell, the oldest viewing point; the Mirador del Carme, adjacent to the cloisters of El Carme; and the Mirador de la Miranda, which is the largest.

TOP 10 EXPERIENCES

Teatre Principal de Maó

Costa d'en Deià, 40

The curtain went up for the first time at Spain's first opera house, the Teatre Principal, on 15th December 1829. The architect Giovanni Palagi designed the building according to the layout and style of 18th century Italian theatres. The opera house underwent a complete refit at the end of the 20th century. Guided tours are available.

Church and cloisters of Sant Francesc

Av. Doctor Guàrdia, s/n

The baroque-style architectural ensemble we see today dates from the 17th and 18th centuries. Following the disentailment of 1835, the convent and cloisters came under municipal ownership (they are now home to the island's museum, the Museu de Menorca). The church is dedicated to Saint Francis and has a single nave and a solid façade with a Romanesque-style portal.

TOP 10 PLACES

Museu de Menorca

Av. Doctor Guàrdia, s/n

The Museu de Menorca is housed in the old Franciscan convent of Maó (17th and 18th centuries). Its galleries cover a surface area of 2,500 m^2 and showcase dozens of pieces spanning prehistoric times to the 20th century. A cultural attraction that is a must for anyone wishing to find out about the history of the island and understand the idiosyncratic nature of Menorcan society.

The clothes, crafts and local food fairs are some of the main attractions of summer nights on Menorca. In Maó, they are held on Tuesday, as part of the initiative *Nits de música al carrer* (nights of music in the street).

Ca n'Oliver

Anuncivay, 2

This mansion is a representative example of 18th-century bourgeois architecture. It houses a museum and interpretation centre focusing on Menorca during British rule. Architectural and artistic highlights include the neoclassical façade and the paintings in the rooms and communal areas.

Fresh-food markets

There are two fresh-food markets in the city centre: the Mercat des Claustre and the Mercat Francesc Femenías – Sa Peixateria. The first stands on the ground floor of the former Carmelite convent and cloisters of Maó (17th-18th centuries), and the second, in a *modernista*-style building designed in the early 20th century by Francesc Femenías i Fábregues. They are both extremely popular today due to the extensive range of food and goods they offer.

***Modernisme* in Maó**

The city of Maó is home to one major landmark in the Catalan art nouveau, or *modernista*, style: the Casa del Poble (Camí des Castell, 31). It was designed by the architect Francesc Femenías i Fábregues who was also responsible for other *modernista*-style projects: the **Casa Mir** (in the photo), the **Casa Martorell** (Plaça Príncep), the **Casa Cardona** (Roser, 1), **Sa Peixateria**, and the industrial buildings **La Eléctrica Mahonesa** (Moll de Ponent, 75) and the **Fàbrica Codina** (Infanta, 203).

MAÓ HARBOUR

Maó harbour is a natural wonder stretching for more than 5km, making it Europe's largest natural port and the second largest port in the world. It is has been a strategic point throughout history from a military, geopolitical and economic point of view. Here are some of its "essential" places.

1

Sant Antoni

An estate also known as The Golden Farm. It has welcomed many eminent visitors, including Empress Sissi of Austria and Kaiser Wilhelm II. However, there is no doubt that the romance between Lord Nelson and Lady Hamilton cemented its legend.

2

Venècia

Venècia is one of the most iconic buildings in Maó harbour. Surrounded by water – hence its name (Venice in Catalan) – this unique house was once the summer home of Sir Richard Branson, and is now an exclusive bar and events venue. You can get there from S'Altra Banda.

3

Illa del Rei

The tiny island, the Illa del Rei, which is also known as The Bloody Island, is steeped in centuries of history: the early Christians built a basilica here in the 5th century, King Alfonso III disembarked here in 1287 and the British built a military hospital in the 18th century.

4

Llatzeret

This was the first isolation hospital in Spain. It opened in the early 18th century to isolate passengers from boats suspected of carrying contagious diseases. It runs guided tours from May to October and is a Cultural Heritage Landmark.

5

La Mola

A masterpiece of military engineering built between 1848 and 1875 on the orders of Queen Isabella II in response to renewed unrest in the western Mediterranean. It is now a major cultural and tourist attraction. For further details, see the section "The fortress trail".

► p. 62

Chapel of Gràcia

The nave of this 15th century chapel, with its ribbed vaults, is one of the few surviving examples of Gothic architecture on Menorca. The portico and façade date from the late 17th and early 18th centuries.

LLUCMAÇANES

This small village, which is part of the municipality of Maó, retains its authentic rural feel. The church dedicated to Saint Cajetan was built in 1885.

SANT CLIMENT

This village is just 4 kilometres from the administrative capital Maó. It was developed relatively recently (19th century), but the community has its own strongly defined personality. History confirms this: prehistoric settlements have been documented here, and the village also has important sites from the early-Christian era (the basilica of Fornàs de Torelló). There are also records of a medieval settlement that predates the current village.

ALAIOR

Alaior is Menorca's third most populous town. Throughout the history of the island, it has played a central role in different areas, and made remarkable contributions to industry, local crafts and education.

ALAIOR

Founded
14th century

Population
10,000 approx.

Surface area
109.8 km²

Density
90 inhabitants/km²

Residential developments
Son Bou
Sant Jaume
Torre-solí
Cala en Porter
Son Vitamina

Alaior beaches
Cala en Porter
Son Bou

www.alaior.org

Church of Santa Eulàlia

Retxats, 4

The church of Santa Eulalia can be traced back to the early 14th century. The original building was destroyed by an earthquake but a new church was built on the site in the late 17th century. However, Santa Eulàlia isn't a baroque church in the strict sense of the word as it retains some Renaissance features. The chapel of El Roser and the doorway, the Portal de Sant Pere, make it well worth a visit.

Town hall

Major, 11

This 16th-century building has been home to the municipal government since 1660, when it was purchased by the old university of Alaior. The building has been named a Historic and Artistic Landmark. A curious fact: an oil press dating from Roman times still stands in one of the rooms.

← The medieval town

The old quarter of Alaior still retains the essence of the medieval village built from 1304 onwards on the site of the former Muslim farmstead of Ihalor. Explore its main streets to appreciate its history.

Escola Graduada des Ramal

Baixamar, 54-56

The Escola Graduada des Ramal opened in 1910 and was the first school on Menorca, and one of the first in Spain, to introduce an educational system based on a streaming system. The building, with its beautiful architecture, is currently home to the school of printmaking, the Centre Internacional d'Art i Gravat de Menorca.

Convent of Sant Diego and Pati de sa Lluna

Es Banyer, s/n

This architectural complex, consisting of a church and cloisters, was built by the Franciscan order in the 17th century. It was home to this religious community until the disentailment of the 19th century when the cloisters, known as the Pati de sa Lluna, were converted into housing. Nowadays, the church hosts cultural events.

Santa Ponça quarry

Camí de sa Costa Blanca

This sandstone quarry stands at the entrance to the Rellotge ravine. It has been abandoned for more than 40 years and was named a Landmark of Cultural Interest in the year 2000. It is well worth a visit.

Basílica de son Bou

Son Bou beach

This early-Christian basilica was built between the 5th and 6th centuries AD on the eastern end of Son Bou beach. It is 25 metres long, 12 metres wide and is thought to have held a congregation of some 300 people, making it one of the biggest religious buildings of the day.

Cova d'en Xoroi

Carrer de sa Cova, 2 (Cala en Porter resort)

This natural grotto, which is a restaurant during the day and a discotheque at night, is one of Menorca's main attractions. It opened in 1964 and five decades later has become one of the most iconic spots in the Mediterranean. Every year it welcomes nearly 100,000 people, a figure that provides ample proof of its powers of attraction.

ES MERCADAL

Es Mercadal stands halfway between Maó and Ciutadella. Its central location has always been its strength, making it a favourite stopping-off point for travellers and a venue for trade fairs, markets and events. It is proud of its status as a hotspot for traditional Menorcan cuisine.

ES MERCADAL

Founded
Early 14th century

Population
5,000 approx.

Surface area
136.9 km²

Density
36.5 inhabitants/km²

Residential developments
Arenal d'en Castell
Son Parc
Coves Noves
Addaia
Na Macaret
Punta Grossa
Platges de Fornells

Es Mercadal beaches
Arenal d'en Castell
Arenal de Son Saura
Cavalleria
Binimel·là
Cala Pregonda

www.aj-esmercadal.org

FORNELLS

Founded
Middle of the 17th century

Population
1,000 approx.

The village of Fornells belongs to the municipality of Es Mercadal.

Church of Sant Martí

Pla de s'Església, 1

The current church, which is dedicated to Saint Martin of Tours, was built between the 18th and 19th centuries on the site of the former parish church. The result is a solid building, with sober lines and austere decorative elements.

S'Aljub

Retxats, 4

The *aljub*, or water-collection tank, is another fine example of British civil architecture. It was built in 1735 on the orders of the British governor Richard Kane to provide water for the troops crossing the island. For further details see the section on "British Menorca".

► p. **36**

Centre Artesanal de Menorca

Av. Metge Camps, s/n

The Centre Artesanal de Menorca is housed in the old military barracks in Es Mercadal and opened at the end of 2005 to provide a platform for the island's craftsmen and women. It stages the permanent exhibition *Menorcan crafts*.

Public estate of S'Arangí

Me-1 road, km 20 marker post

The public estate of S'Arangí opened to the public in 2012 and is owned by the government of the Balearic Islands. It has 3 km of hiking trails and three viewing points overlooking Toro, Es Mercadal and Fornells, as well as a conservation area with protected flora and a leisure area.

Cavalleria

The northern peninsula of Cavalleria is one of the most interesting spots on Menorca in terms of its natural scenery, history and culture. The Cavalleria beaches, Sanitja harbour, the archaeological site at Sanisera, the Cavalleria lighthouse and the interpretation centre, the Centre de Interpretació de la Costa Nord de Menorca, provide ample proof of this.

Sanitja

Cavalleria peninsula

Es Mercadal has three natural harbours: Fornells (p. 58), Addaia and Sanitja. The latter is situated in a special protection area and remains completely unspoilt, giving it a bucolic and romantic atmosphere. The Roman settlement of Sanisera is located just a few metres from here.

El Toro

Menorca is a low-lying island and its highest mountain, which stands 358 metres high, is El Toro. From the top, with its shrine to the Virgin, the Mare de Déu del Toro (16th century), you can enjoy fantastic panoramic views of most of the island, particularly the north and west. On a clear day you can make out the neighbouring island of Mallorca.

FORNELLS

Fornells is the only village on the northern coast of Menorca. Its origins date back to the 17th century, when the castle of Sant Antoni was built. A combination of the fishing tradition and tourism has made Fornells one of the island's culinary hotspots. It belongs to the municipality of Es Mercadal.

Lobster, the queen of Menorcan cuisine

The spiny lobster is the queen of Menorcan cuisine. A humble dish, the lobster stew, or *caldereta de langosta*, has become a tourist experience in its own right. For further details, see the chapter "Made in Menorca".

► p. **152**

Fornells tower

Punta de sa Torre

This is one of biggest and best-preserved defence towers on the island. It was planned and built by the British in 1802 and was restored and opened to the public in the year 2000. It is well worth a visit.

▸ p. **62**

Mola de Fornells

Across the bay from Fornells stretches La Mola, an unspoilt peninsula which stands 122 metres above sea level at its northernmost tip. It is difficult to get to and this explains its beautiful scenery and environmental worth. Erosion of the massif has given rise to two caves that are very popular with divers and potholers: the Cova dels Anglesos and the Cova de Na Polida.

Hartung and Bergman

The artists Hans Hartung and Anna-Eva Bergman came to Menorca in 1932 believing they had found a paradise where they could give free rein to their creativity. Their house in Cala Tirant is arguably the first example of contemporary architecture on the Balearic Islands.

THE FORTRESS TRAIL

Castles, fortresses, watchtowers, artillery towers, military batteries, gunpowder magazines and trenches give a good account of Menorca's military past. Here is a list of some of the most important.

Fort Marlborough

Es Castell

Fort Marlborough was built between 1710 and 1726 and is one of the most spectacular strongholds built by the British on the island. Its architecture is particularly unusual as a large area of the fort has been dug out of the rock and can't be seen from the outside. There is an exhibition recreating life at the fort, the sieges it endured, and the history of Menorca and Europe in the 18th century.

La Mola

Maó harbour

The fortress of La Mola is the most imposing building on the fortress trail. It was built between 1848 and 1875 on the orders of Queen Isabella II in response to renewed tensions in the Mediterranean and is a major feat of military engineering. It was one of the largest forts in Europe in the 19th century but became obsolete shortly after it came into use due to the evolution of artillery technology. La Mola is currently a well-known cultural and tourist attraction.

Fortress cities

Ciutadella contains two important sections of the medieval walls: the Bastió de sa Font, which is now home to the Museu Municipal de Ciutadella, and the Bastió des Governador (p. 78). In Maó, the Portal de Sant Roc still stands. It was one of the five gates into the medieval city (p. 41).

Defence towers

There are 14 defence towers on Menorca, 11 of them are British in origin: the Stuart Tower, also known as the Torre d'en Penjat, or hanged man's tower, Cala Teulera, La Princesa, Sant Felipet, Sa Mesquida, Rambla, Fornells, Es Castellar, Sanitja, Ses Sargantanes and Cala Molí. The remaining three are Spanish in origin: Sant Nicolau, Son Ganxo and Alcalfar.

Castle of Sant Felip

Es Castell

Little remains except the foundations of the castle built in the middle of the 16th century on the orders of King Philip II. It was designed to protect the population from attacks during a time of major upheavals but it didn't survive beyond the late 18th century when King Carlos III ordered its demolition. The castle formed the original nucleus of the village of El Castell.

Castle of Sant Antoni

Fornells

The history of this castle is similar to that of Sant Felip. It was built between 1637 and 1677 to protect the local population from the pirate attacks that took place from the 16th to the 17th centuries. It was also destroyed on the orders of King Carlos III at the end of the 18th century. A walkway has been placed around the site to make it more accessible for visitors.

Castle of Santa Àgueda

Ferreries

This is one of the few surviving relics from the period of Moorish rule (10th-13th centuries). It was built on the island's third-tallest peak (Santa Àgueda, 264 m). The path leading to the castle retains its original stone paving.

ES MIGJORN GRAN

This small town exudes the essence of Menorca. It is a peaceful spot where time seems to have stood still. Although it is the newest town on the island, it has a great many archaeological sites that confirm the existence of human settlements from late prehistoric times.

ES MIGJORN GRAN

Founded
Middle of the 18th century (separated from Es Mercadal and awarded town status in 1989)

Population
1,500 approx.

Surface area
31.4 km^2

Density
47.7 inhabitants/km^2

Residential developments
Sant Tomàs

Es Migjorn Gran beaches
Cala Trebalúger
Cala Fustam
Cala Escorxada
Binigaus

www.ajesmigjorn.org

Long-lived locals

Es Migjorn Gran holds the secret to long life. One of its inhabitants, Joan Riudavets Moll, celebrated his 114th birthday in 2004, making him the oldest man in the world after the death of Yukichi Chiganji. His brother Pere lived to the age of 104.

Church of Sant Cristòfol

Sant Llorenç, 6

The church, with its single nave and interconnecting side chapels, was begun in 1768 as an initiative of the local residents in this rural area. Just like the other municipalities on the island, the church was the first building in the town.

Gran Migjornale

Es Migjorn was the first town on Menorca to take art outside galleries into public spaces and houses. The initiative, known as Gran Migjornale, is held in the summer every two years.

Cova des Coloms

Camí de sa Malagarba - Binigaus ravine

The Cova des Coloms, known as 'The Cathedral' because of its size (300 m deep and 24 m high), is a natural cave in the Binigaus ravine. The objects found inside suggest that it was used as a shrine or place of religious pilgrimage during the Talayotic period.

Library

Sant Cristòfol, 9

The municipal library specialises in folklore and popular culture. It is home to the bequest of Francesc Camps i Mercadal (1852-1929), known as Francesc d'Albranca, a doctor by profession, scholar and amateur folklorist.

FERRERIES

The Catalan writer Josep Pla described Ferreries as "the whitest town in the world". Perceptions apart, it is true that Ferreries is the highest town of them all and this may be the reason why it has so much light. It is well worth stopping off here to explore the streets in the centre and enjoy the skills of its master craftsmen and women.

FERRERIES

Founded
Late 13th century (separated from Es Mercadal in 1989)

Population
4,500 approx.

Surface area
66 km²

Density
73.9 inhabitants/km²

Residential developments
Cala Galdana
Els Alocs

Ferreries beaches
Cala Galdana
Cala Mitjana and Mitjaneta

www.ajferreries.org

Church of Sant Bartomeu

Pla de l'Església

This neoclassical church (18th century) consists of a single, cross-shaped nave with a barrel-vaulted ceiling. The original doorway overlooks the side street. Standing on the same square is the Casa de ses Voltes, one of the oldest buildings in the town which houses council offices.

Plaça de sa Peixateria

Sant Llorenç, 6

At the top of Ferreries, this tiny cobbled square is one of the most charming spots in the town. It takes its name from the former fishmongers' building, which stands adjacent to a water-collector known as Ses Fonts de Prop.

Sa Rovellada

It isn't easy to find high points from which to admire the Menorcan landscape. That's why we recommend you go on this 25-minute walk to the top of Sa Rovellada where you'll find the small chapel dedicated to the Virgin Mary. The entrance is signposted after you have crossed a stream.

Santa Àgueda

This is the third-highest mountain on the island (264 m) after El Toro and S'Enclusa. At the top you'll find the ruins of an ancient Moorish castle (which is likely to have been abandoned in the 14th century). The path leading to the castle retains the original stone paving.

S'Enclusa

S'Enclusa (275 m) is the site of an American military base that was operational from 1965 until 1993. Since 2007, it has been owned by the government, the Consell de Menorca, which plans to turn the buildings into an interpretation centre for the Biosphere Reserve.

Algendar ravine

The south of Menorca is criss-crossed by ravines featuring breathtaking natural scenery. The most important is Algendar which stretches for almost 7km and emerges onto the spectacular beach at Cala Galdana. Two caves – the Cova Murada and the Cova des Càrritx – contain prehistoric relics.

CIUTADELLA

Ciutadella, the most stately city, was, for centuries, the undisputed centre of political, economic, cultural and ecclesiastical power on Menorca. The traces of this dominance still endure in the city's civil and religious architecture and urban layout. Here are some of the main places of interest.

CIUTADELLA

Founded
3rd century BC

Population
30,000 approx.

Surface area
186.3 km²

Density
160 inhabitants/km²

Residential developments
Cala en Blanes
Cales Piques
Sa Caleta
Santandria
Cala Blanca
Cala en Bosc
Son Xoriguer
Cala Morell
Serpentona

Ciutadella beaches
Cala Pilar
Algaiarens
Cala en Blanes
Cala Blanca
Cala en Bosc
Son Xoriguer
Son Saura - Cala des Talaier
Cala en Turqueta
Macarella and Macarelleta

www.ajciutadella.org

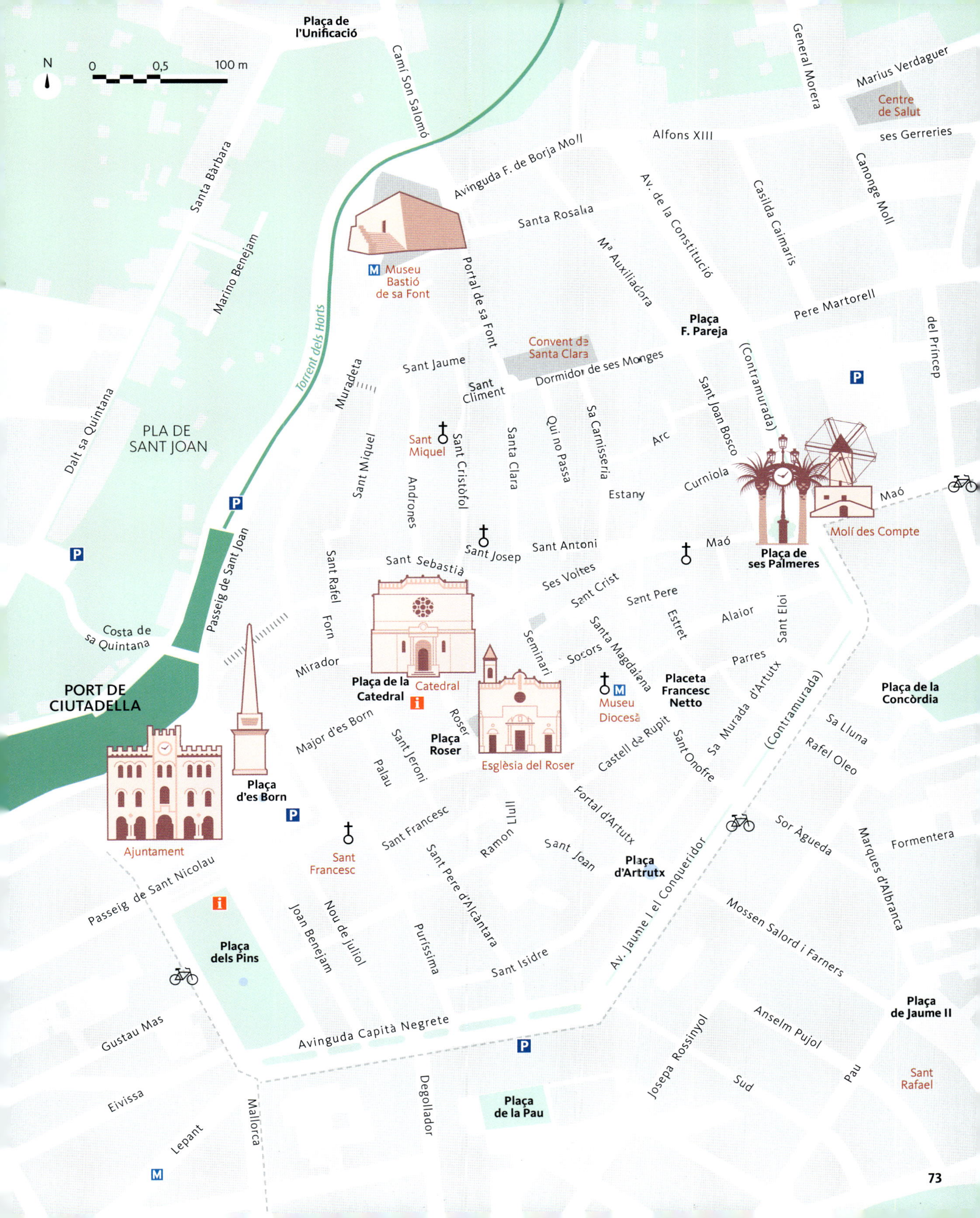
N
0
0,5
100 m
Plaça de l'Unificació
Camí Son Salomó
General Morera
Marius Verdaguer
Centre de Salut
Alfons XIII
ses Gerreries
Avinguda F. de Borja Moll
Santa Bàrbara
Marino Benejam
Torrent dels Horts
Museu Bastió de sa Font
Santa Rosalia
Av. de la Constitució
Casilda Caimaris
Canonge Moll
Mª Auxiliadora
Portal de sa Font
Pere Martorell
del Príncep
Plaça F. Pareja
Convent de Santa Clara
Dormidor de ses Monges
(Contramurada)
Sant Jaume
Sant Climent
Muradeta
Dalt sa Quintana
PLA DE SANT JOAN
Sant Miquel
Sant Cristòfol
Santa Clara
Qui no Passa
Sa Carnisseria
Sant Joan Bosco
Arc
Curniola
Estany
Andrones
Maó
Molí des Compte
Sant Josep
Sant Antoni
Maó
Plaça de ses Palmeres
Passeig de Sant Joan
Sant Rafel
Sant Sebastià
Ses Voltes
Sant Crist
Sant Pere
Alaior
Sant Eloi
Estret
Costa de sa Quintana
Forn
Seminari
Socors
Santa Magdalena
Parres
Mirador
PORT DE CIUTADELLA
Plaça de la Catedral
Catedral
Placeta Francesc Netto
Museu Diocesà
Plaça de la Concòrdia
Sa Murada d'Artutx
(Contramurada)
Sa Lluna
Major d'es Born
Roser
Sant Jeroni
Plaça Roser
Castell de Rupit
Sant Onofre
Rafel Oleo
Palau
Església del Roser
Plaça d'es Born
Ajuntament
Fortal d'Artutx
Sant Francesc
Ramon Llull
Sor Àgueda
Marques d'Albranca
Formentera
Sant Joan
Plaça d'Artrutx
Passeig de Sant Nicolau
Sant Pere d'Alcàntara
Av. Jaume I el Conqueridor
Mossen Salord i Farners
Plaça dels Pins
Joan Benejam
Nou de juliol
Puríssima
Sant Isidre
Plaça de Jaume II
Gustau Mas
Avinguda Capità Negrete
Anselm Pujol
Josepa Rossinyol
Sud
Pau
Sant Rafael
Eivissa
Degollador
Mallorca
Plaça de la Pau
Lepant

Historic centre

Ciutadella's slow and late urban growth (the medieval walls stood until the 19th century) accounts for the excellent state of repair of its historic centre. Its irregular layout means that tracing a route through its streets is no easy task. Nevertheless, the existence of two clearly defined arteries makes it simpler: the first runs from east to west and connects the Portal de Maó and the Portal d'en Sales, and the second runs from north to south and connects the Portal de Sa Font and Artrutx.

Church of El Roser

This 17th-century church with a single nave and side chapels is now used as a gallery run by the city council. The building is attributed to the Amorós brothers who designed the few surviving examples of baroque architecture on the island.

TOP 10 PLACES

The cathedral

This is the main place of worship on the island. Built from the 13th to 14th centuries in the Catalan Gothic style, it stands on the site of the great synagogue in the former Medina. The foot of the bell tower, which was also the base of the ancient minaret, is the only Muslim relic to have survived. The cathedral was restored in the 16th and 19th centuries. The neoclassical-style door on the main façade covers the original Gothic one. There are two other outstanding buildings in the square: La Seixantina and the Casa Olivar.

Jewish Quarter

Few traces remain of Ciutadella's Jewish Quarter and the irregular layout of some of the streets (Sant Jeroni, Sant Francesc and Palau) are the only reminders of the period. The synagogue, now vanished, stood on Carrer Sant Jeroni.

Ses Voltes

This is one of Ciutadella's best-known streets. The vaulted arcades are its most distinctive feature. They are thought to be ancient in origin, although we don't know when they were planned and who designed them. At the eastern end of the street stands the Plaça Nova, which marked the boundary of the Medina Manurqa. A section of the Moorish arcades still stands on one side of the square.

Es Be

Matías Quetglas's small bronze sculpture stands on a concrete plinth halfway along Ses Voltes. It represents the city's main festival in the form of a ram bearing the flag of Saint John.

Plaça des Born

This is the nerve centre of the city. It stands at the end of the east-west route and was once the site of the gardens of the Royal Palace of the Medina Manurqa. Following the Christian conquest of the island (13th century), the site was converted into a parade ground. The obelisk was erected in 1857 in memory of the city's resistance to the attack perpetrated by the Franco-Ottoman army on 9th July 1558, known locally as "s'any de sa desgràcia" (the year of the disaster).

Church of Sant Francesc

Plaça des Born, 8

The church dates back to the time of the Christian conquest of the island (13th century) although the building we see today was built following the Turkish invasion (16th-17th centuries). The church was part of an architectural complex comprising a convent an allotment that no longer exist.

Fortified city

The Bastió des Governador, situated behind city hall, and the Bastió de sa Font are the only surviving relics of the medieval city walls. There was originally a fortification of this type above each of the five gates into the city.

► p. 63

Bastió de sa Font

Plaça de sa Font, s/n

The Bastió de sa Font currently houses the Museu Municipal de Ciutadella. It was built in the 17th century to reinforce the city walls. The museum showcases many archaeological exhibits that tell us about Menorca's early history, from prehistoric times to the Muslim and early-Christian eras.

The Amorós architects

The Amorós family originally hailed from Mallorca and had a marked influence on the architecture of Ciutadella between the 17th and 18th centuries. Their buildings are among the most important examples of Menorcan baroque architecture, and include the church of El Roser, the gallery in the church of Sant Francesc and the Can Saura Miret mansion.

Ciutadella harbour

This is one of the most historic harbours on the Balearic Islands, and, like Maó, has played a decisive role in the growth of the city throughout its history. The Baixamar area retains the charm of a quayside from bygone years and has a great choice of bars and restaurants. Inside the harbour, the Pla de Sant Joan is a nightlife hotspot.

Convent of Santa Clara

Portal de sa Font, 2

Like many of the religious and civil buildings in the city, the convent of Sant Clara fell victim to the brutal Turkish attacks in the 16th century. It was rebuilt in the baroque style in the 17th century but suffered another setback during the Spanish Civil War (1936-1939). The foundation stone of the current building was laid in 1946.

Sant Joan de Missa

Camí de Sant Joan de Missa, s/n

A small rural church dating back to the early 14th century. The simple outline of the church is enhanced by its brilliant white colour and bell gable. It plays a central role during the festival of Sant Joan.

Plaça de la Llibertat

This charming little square, which is also known as the Plaça des Mercat, is one of the most popular places in the city. People come here to do their shopping, have a drink and a bite to eat. The fishmongers' and butchers' galleries, designed by the architect Ramon Cavaller, are the only examples of cast-iron architecture in Ciutadella (19th century). Nearby, you'll find the Casa de Cultura and municipal library, housed in an 18th-century building once used as a hospital and boarding school for orphans.

Castle of Sant Nicolau

This defence tower was built at the end of the 17th century to keep watch over the entrance to Ciutadella harbour and protect it from possible attacks. It is part of the network of military towers dotted along the Menorcan coast (p. 63). This one is the most elegant: it has an octagonal floor plan and a moat around its perimeter, which is 2 metres deep.

► p. **63**

TRADITIONAL MENORCA

Menorca is a land of deeply rooted traditions. Over the centuries, Menorcans have preserved countless customs and expressions of their culture. The local festivals dedicated to the patron saints of each municipality are among the most representative, with **Sant Joan** (Ciutadella, 23rd-24th June) as the main event. Horses, traditional dances, and processions of *gegants* (giant figures with papier-mâché heads dressed in different costumes) and *capgrossos* (small figures wearing oversized papier-mâché heads) ... In summer, the towns and villages are a lively blend of folklore. The year's festival calendar also incudes other important events, including the island's feast day, the **Diada del Poble de Menorca** (17th January), carnival and Holy Week

Diada del Poble de Menorca (17th January). On the eve of Sant Antoni people hold traditional *torrades populars*: community dinners where they eat the local spicy sausage, *sobrassada*, and other cured sausages grilled over embers.

The traditional Menorcan dances are the **fandango**, the **jota**, the **bolero** and the ***ball des còssil***.

The festivals of Sant Joan are the oldest on the island and can be traced back to the Middle Ages.

Menorca has its own breed of horse characterised by its jet-black coat, slender, muscular appearance and even temperament.

The tradition of **gegants i capgrossos** dates back to the early 20th century and has only become established on the eastern side of the island.

HEAVEN ON EARTH

The coast of **MENORCA** stretches for 220 km and features more than 100 coves and beaches of breathtaking beauty, many of them completely unspoilt. What makes the island so wonderful is the fact that it has escaped the threat of urban development that has altered so much of the Mediterranean. It has also led to Menorca being awarded Biosphere Reserve status. In this chapter we will visit some of the most representative coves and beaches in the north and south of the island: the former is more rugged with the predominance of clay and slate, whereas the latter is more lush with pine glades, white sands and crystal-clear waters. Won't you join us?

MENORCA'S BEST BEACHES AND COVES

NORTHERN COAST

1 Cala Mesquida
2 Es Grau
3 Cala des Tamarells
4 Arenal de Morella
5 Arenal de Capifort
6 S'Enclusa
7 Mongofre
8 Arenal d'en Castell
9 Arenal de Son Saura
10 Cavalleria
11 Binimel·là
12 Cala Pregonda-s'Alairó
13 Cala Pilar
14 Cala d'Algaiarens
15 Cala en Blanes

SOUTHERN COAST

16 Cala Blanca
17 Cala en Bosc
18 Son Xoriguer
19 Son Saura-Cala des Talaier
20 Cala en Turqueta
21 Cala Macarella-Cala Macarelleta
22 Cala Galdana
23 Cala Trebalúger
24 Cala Fustam-Cala Escorxada
25 Binigaus-Binicodrell
26 Son Bou
27 Cala en Porter
28 Cala de Binidalí
29 Cala de Binibèquer
30 Punta Prima

1 CALA MESQUIDA

39.9155, 4.2866

This is the nearest cove to the city of Maó (6.5 km). To get there you have to go through the traditional village of Sa Mesquida, where the Maó locals go to spend the summer and which retains the atmosphere of a fishing village of yesteryear. The main beach is 300 metres long and 50 metres wide. It is flanked by two mounds: Es Pa Gros, which stands 60 metres high, and Punta de sa Creueta, which is surmounted by a watchtower built by the British in the late 18th century.

Racó de sa Creueta.

2 ES GRAU

39.9503, 4.2657

This is one of the longest beaches on the northern coast. Its shallow, calm waters, services and proximity to the holiday resort of Es Grau make it a favourite with families. The beach overlooks the saltwater lake of Albufera des Grau, the centrepiece of the natural park of the same name and the heart of the Biosphere Reserve. The lake and beach are connected by a stream: the Gola de s'Albufera. We recommend you take one of the signposted routes to discover the rich biodiversity of the area.

S'Albufera des Grau.

THE ALBUFERA DES GRAU NATURAL PARK COVERS A SURFACE AREA OF 5,000 HECTARES BETWEEN ES GRAU AND ADDAIA HARBOUR. THE MOST IMPORTANT AREAS ARE ALBUFERA, ILLA D'EN COLOM AND THE FAVÀRITX PROMONTORY.

3 ARENAL D'EN MORO

39.5749, 4.1628

The Illa d'en Colom is the largest island on Menorca. It covers a surface area of 59 ha and has two beaches: Cala Tamarells and Arenal d'en Moro. In summer you will often see pleasure boats moored just off the shore. This is one of the most interesting natural areas on the island.

ISLANDS WITHIN AN ISLAND

Menorca has its satellites: small islands. The 220 km of coastline is home to more than 30 of these islands, including four in Maó harbour. The best known, due to their geographical features and wealth of flora and fauna, are the **Illa d'en Colom** and the **Illa de l'Aire**. There are many more, including **d'en Tosqueta**, **des Porros**, **ses Sargantanes** and **ses Bledes**. A whole world waiting to be discovered.

Illa de l'Aire

Punta Prima, (Sant Lluís)

This little island, standing off the coast of Sant Lluís, covers an area of just over 30 ha. It is a site of environmental importance as it is the natural habitat of the endemic black lizard, known as Lilford's wall lizard (*Podarcis lilfordi lilfordi*). It is also a stopover site for migratory birds and proposals have been made to turn the island into a nature reserve.

Illa d'en Colom

Es Grau, (Maó)

The Illa d'en Colom is the largest island on Menorca and covers a surface area of 59 ha. It is one of the most interesting natural areas on the island, in part because it is the habitat of a species of lizard endemic to the Balearic Islands – Lilford's wall lizard (*Podarcis lilfordi lilfordi*) – which is only found on some of the smaller islands and Cabrera. The subspecies, *Podarcis lilfordi baleárica*, lives on the Illa d'en Colom.

Illes d'Addaia

The small islands in Addaia harbour (Illa Gran, Illa Petita and Illa de ses Àguiles) make up one of the five natural reserves in the Albufera des Grau Natural Park, together with the Illa d'en Colom, S'Estany, the wetlands of Morella and Es Prat. The Illes d'Addaia stand on the western boundary of the natural park.

4 ARENAL DE MORELLA (Cala Tortuga)

39.9886, 4.2554

The cove Arenal de Morella, which is also known as Cala Tortuga, is one of the most beautiful spots on the Maó coast. It is a protected area within the Albufera des Grau Natural Park and this explains why its dunes and vegetation, which mostly consists of tamarinds, are so well preserved. Behind the cove is a coastal lagoon covering an area of 2.5 ha. You can get here along the bridle path, the Camí des Cavalls, from Es Grau and the Favàritx road.

Please note: In high season the beach becomes very crowded. To get there, you have to take the shuttle bus that connects Maó with Favàritx. More information: www.mou-tmenorca.com

View of Favàritx lighthouse from the beach.

5 ARENAL DE CAPIFORT (Cala Presili)

39.9922, 4.2551

These sands have a similar structure, geological composition, vegetation and surrounding landscape as Arenal de Morella. However, in this case, large numbers of visitors have caused damage to the coastal plant life. Rocky outcrops at both ends of the cove, with the imposing lighthouse perched on top of Cap Favàritx, protect it from the tramontana winds. The seabed, with its fine, white sands, means both beaches – Capifort and Morella – resemble the beaches on the south of the island. They are perfect for bathing.

6 S'ENCLUSA

39.9978, 4.2208

Two beaches shelter beneath the Punta de S'Enclusa: S'Enclusa and Mongofre. They are both more than 100 metres long. Before you get to the first, S'Enclusa, you will come to Es Caló des Peix, or S'Arenalet, a small cove with similar features to its neighbours. Next to it, nestling between rocky promontories dotted with native plants, stands S'Enclusa. Although it doesn't attract many bathers, it is extremely popular with pleasure boats in summer.

Weaving the Land, installation by Núria Roman on Mongofre.

7 S'ARENALET DE MONGROFE

40.0001, 4.2174

Mongofre beach is easily reached from S'Enclusa. It is a semi-circular, east-facing inlet protected from the northern wind, making it a favourite stop-off point for boats. Like neighbouring S'Enclusa, Mongofre has a wealth of native plant species. It has one of the best-preserved dune systems on the island. The beach backs onto a forest of savin junipers and pines that provide shelter for bathers and hikers on the hottest days.

8 ARENAL D'EN CASTELL

40.0223, 4.1830

At almost 650 metres long and 20 metres wide, this is one of the longest beaches on Menorca. It is located in one of the most popular resorts on the northern coast, and its fine, white sand and crystal-clear, shallow waters, as well as the services it offers, make it particularly popular with families. The fact that it is easily accessible and located close to the hotels and houses in the resort, explain the high numbers of bathers throughout the season. This horseshoe-shaped beach and the narrow, rocky mouth of the bay give this coastal landscape its own unique personality.

Trip to Cala Pudent

From Son Saura you can walk to the tucked-away cove Cala Pudent, a small inlet with shallow waters set among completely unspoilt scenery. On the way, you'll discover beautiful spots like the one shown in the photo.

9 ARENAL DE SON SAURA

40.0336, 4.1623

This medium-sized beach (330 metres long and 60 metres wide) is also known as the Arenal de s'Olla, or Son Parc, after the resort that has developed around it. It has one of the best-preserved dune systems on the Menorcan coast. Two low-lying crags, one on each side, act as natural breakwaters although they don't protect the beach from the northerly wind. Building has had a low impact on the site and centres on the right-hand side of the beach. Together with Arenal d'en Castell, it has the same characteristics as the beaches in the south of the island: fine, white sand and turquoise waters

LIGHTHOUSES

Menorca has seven lighthouses: three of them located in the municipality of Ciutadella (**Punta Nati**, **Artrutx** and **Sa Farola**), two in Maó (**Favàritx** and **Sant Carles**), one in Es Mercadal (**Cavalleria**) and one in Sant Lluís (**Illa de l'Aire**). The oldest lighthouse of the seven is Cavalleria, which was built in 1857 to reduce the number of accidents and shipwrecks off the northern coast. Two years later, Artrutx lighthouse, on the south-east coast, became operational, and the Illa de l'Aire lighthouse opened in 1860. The more recent ones are Punta Nati, built in 1910 to prevent tragedies such as the shipwreck of the steamer *General Chanzy*, in which 156 people died, and Favàritx, which opened in 1922.

Cavalleria lighthouse.

10 CAVALLERIA

40.0599, 4.0762

Sheltered by Cap de Cavalleria, Menorca's most northerly promontory with cliffs standing 80 metres above sea level, Cavalleria and Ferragut beaches and the neighbouring Cala Roja, have become one of the most imposing sights on the northern coast of Menorca. The contrast between the transparent waters, golden sands and red clayey hills are contributing factors.

Please note: Although they may seem harmless, mud baths cause severe erosion.

Sanitja

Situated at the start of the Cavalleria peninsula, Sanitja combines the appeal of history –it houses the remains of a Roman settlement – with beautiful scenery and a wealth of ethnographic elements. An essential place on Menorca.

11 BINIMEL·LÀ

40.0521, 4.0532

An unspoilt beach which is almost 300 metres long and 40 metres wide. You can get there by car or on foot along the bridle path, the Camí de Cavalls. To reach the sea from the car park you have to bypass a system of dunes and a stream which is a habitat for different bird species. The fact that the tourist beach of Cala Pregonda is nearby means that Binimel·là isn't especially overcrowded. On the right-hand shore there are three coves that are perfect for bathing: Cova des Punt, Caleta de na Elisabet and Punta de Binimel·là. A unique spot.

THE NORTH MENORCA MARINE RESERVE COVERS AN AREA OF 5,119 HECTARES BETWEEN FORNELLS AND CAP GROS (CIUTADELLA). THE RESERVE WAS SET UP IN ORDER TO ENSURE THE NATURAL REGENERATION OF RESOURCES AND PRESERVE THE MOST REPRESENTATIVE ECOSYSTEMS.

12 CALA PREGONDA

39.9155, 4.2866

One of the jewels of the Menorcan coast and, arguably, the entire Mediterranean. The whimsical interplay of colours created by the clays, volcanic rocks and vivid blue of the sea makes it a unique spot. Mike Oldfield was aware of this and used a photo of the cove and its unique reefs on the cover of his album *Incantations* (1978). Before you reach Cala Pregonda you'll pass through S'Alairó, a beach with similar characteristics which has peaceful bathing areas tucked away at one end.

13 CALA PILAR

40.0514, 3.9785

The contrasting colours are the most striking thing about this corner of the northern coast: the red rocks and earth, the golden sands, the green vegetation and the blue sea. A wooden walkway leads down to the beach to lessen the impact of visitors. This medium-sized cove is part of the public estate of Alfurí de Dalt, one of the most interesting natural sites on Menorca. You can get here on foot from the Alfurí car park (45 minutes) or from Els Alocs (30 minutes). Both of them can be reached on the Me-1 road.

Dune systems

Coastal dunes are fragile ecosystems of great geological and environmental value. In recent decades they have suffered from the effects of human pressure, particularly as a result of the development of the coastline. Menorca has some of the best-preserved dune systems on the Balearic Islands as a result of a territorial policy that sets out to protect them.

14 CALA D'ALGAIARENS (La Vall)

40.0485, 3.9217

This large cove consists of the beaches of Es Tancats and Es Bot, which are reached easily from two public car parks. This is undoubtedly one of the most beautiful areas on the Menorcan coast due to the perfect combination of white sand, turquoise waters and intense green of the surrounding woodland. La Vall boasts stunning landscapes with a wealth of flora and fauna and is an environmentally protected area. To bear in mind: the beach has one of the largest and best-preserved dune systems in the Balearic Islands.

Sa Bassa Verda

Sa Bassa Verda is a very beautiful, temporary pond situated just a short distance away from the Algaiarens beaches. Together with 25 other ponds on the island, it is part of a European Union project to preserve these habitats.

15 CALA EN BLANES

40.0003, 3.8129

Cala en Blanes was one of the first purpose-built tourist resorts on Menorca and epitomises all the beaches on the west side of the island: a narrow strip of fine, white sand, turquoise waters, a surrounding resort and all kinds of services. The palm grove is one of the unique features of the cove and is used as a picnic area by locals and bathers.

FURTHER SOUTH, IN CALA BLANCA, YOU'LL FIND THE S'AIGUA AND NA MAGARÉ CAVES. THEY ARE WIDE GROTTOES WITH STALACTITES AND STALAGMITES AND HAVE ONE OF THE LARGEST UNDERGROUND LAKES IN SPAIN. THEY ARE EXPECTED TO OPEN TO THE PUBLIC SHORTLY.

16 CALA EN BOSC

39.9259, 3.8374

If you start the route from Ciutadella, Cala en Bosch is the first cove you come to on the southern coast of Menorca. Standing between Cap d'Artrutx and Punta de sa Guarda, it retains some of the characteristics of the southern bathing areas, such as the fine, white sand and deep-turquoise waters. Unlike the virgin beaches, the white pine and ilex groves have been replaced by buildings. The indoor lagoon on the right-hand shore has been converted into a marina.

17 SON XORIGUER

39.9251, 3.8411

Son Xoriguer beach is similar to the neighbouring Cala en Bosc, and marks the boundary between the built-up southern coast of Ciutadella, and the unspoilt coast. Building has had the greatest impact on the western part and back of this large beach, leaving the area on the left free. One of the most important protected natural areas on the island begins here and extends as far as Cala Galdana, in Ferreries.

Cova dels Pardals

The small white house on the eastern tip of Cala Parejals has a flight of steps leading down to the Cova dels Pardals. The cave, with its floor carved out to form a landing stage, is thought to have been used to store smuggled goods in the past. It is now a wonderful, peaceful bathing area.

18 SON SAURA AND ES TALAIER

39.9265, 3.8962

Es Banyuls and Bellavista are two large beaches separated by a line of rocks known as the 'lloses des governador' (governor's slabs). The beaches are known collectively as Son Saura. Their size, ease of access and superb waters make them especially popular. The bridle path, the Camí de Cavalls, runs behind the beaches, near the wetland area of Prat de Bellavista, and winds up the craggy coast as far as Es Talaier, a paradise-like cove with fine white sand, crystal-clear waters and a leafy pine grove at the rear. It is named after the person who once guarded the Artrutx watchtower (17th century).

Neptune grass

The beaches of Son Saura are frequently covered in a carpet of Neptune grass (*Posidonia oceanica*). It is an aquatic plant (not a seaweed) that plays an important role in protecting the coast from possible erosion. It is also a bioindicator for water quality, meaning it is a huge mistake to assume that it pollutes the beaches.

An interesting fact: The Balearic island of Formentera has a Neptune grass meadow stretching for more than 8km that dates back 100,000 years. It is thought to be the oldest living organism on earth.

19 CALA EN TURQUETA

39.9320, 3.9149

Cala en Turqueta is one of the most popular unspoilt beaches on Menorca, together with Macarella, Macarelleta and Cala Mitjana. From here to Binigaus, in Es Migjorn Gran, you'll find a string of heavenly beaches with no buildings whatsoever, with just one exception: the majestic Cala Galdana. What's its appeal? The clean, deep-turquoise waters, the fine, white sand, the dense woodland and lack of buildings.

20 MACARELLA AND MACARELLETA

39.9382, 3.9371

The Macarella and Macarelleta coves are two of Menorca's main attractions and similar to the neighbouring Cala en Turqueta. They captivate visitors with their broad colour palette, the beautiful natural scenery of the ravine and the imposing cliffs that guard them. The islanders' forebears must have taken these aspects into account when they placed their burial caves here.

Please note: In high season the beach becomes very crowded. To get there, you have to take the shuttle bus that connects Ciutadella with the unspoilt coves on the southern coast. More information: www.mou-tmenorca.com

MENORCA HAS A WIDE NETWORK OF COASTAL PATHS IN ADDITION TO THE CAMÍ DE CAVALLS. THEY ARE MARKED BY WOODEN POSTS AND ALLOW YOU TO EXPLORE MOST OF THE COAST ON FOOT, BY BIKE OR ON HORSEBACK.

21 CALA GALDANA

39.9373, 3.9600

In this secluded spot on the southern coast between Morro de Ponent and the imposing Penyal Vermell, a sea inlet forms a beach in the shape of a large shell. The western side of the cove stands at the mouth of the Algendar ravine where the stream of the same name flows into the sea, creating a wetland area that has been adapted as a jetty. Cala Galdana is considered the most beautiful cove on Menorca despite the buildings that occupy almost all of this natural arch. A gift to nature with all kinds of amenities for visitors.

22 MITJANA AND MITJANETA

39.9341, 3.9723

Together with Macarella, Macarelleta and Cala en Turqueta, these are the unspoilt coves that are most popular with tourists. They have almost identical features: beaches of fine, white sand, a sandy sea bed which, together with the quality of the water, account for the turquoise colour of the sea, dense pine groves on the path leading to the coves and on the top of the cliffs that protect them, and no hint of building around them. Near Mitjaneta, the tiny cove reached by a flight of steps on the right of Mitjana, you can see a small sandstone quarry which is no longer in use. You'll often see youngsters diving off the cliff on the east side of Mitjana.

Cala Mitjaneta
A tiny cove with fine, white sand reached by a wooden flight of steps from neighbouring Mitjana. In this sheltered spot, six people are a crowd.

23 CALA TREBALÚGER

39.9309, 3.9890

From the west, Trebalúger is the first beach in Es Migjorn Gran, the municipality that is proud to have four of the finest virgin coves on Menorca: Trebalúger itself, Cala Fustam, Cala Escorxada and Binigaus. Trebalúger has similar characteristics to Macarella, Macarelleta, Turqueta and Mitjana and, in addition to its pure greens, blues and whites, has a distinctive feature: it stands at the mouth of the Trebáluger ravine which gives it a unique appearance. Trebalúger is a little more isolated than the others, making it less crowded in high season. It is well worth a visit.

There are two lovely surprises along the Menorcan coast between Trebalúger and Binigaus: the Fustam and Escorxada coves. A wonderful reward for anyone wishing to explore this interesting coastal trail.

24 FUSTAM AND ESCORXADA

39.9257, 4.0007

Two gems on the southern coast of Menorca. Separated by the headland of Sant Antoni and less than 1 km apart, Fustam and Escorxada amaze visitors with their crystal-clear waters and surrounding dense woodland. It isn't difficult to reach these beaches on foot but you should wear suitable footwear as the path runs close to the sea and is rocky in places. It takes 45 minutes to reach Cala Escorxada from Binigaus and another 10 minutes to get to Cala Fustam. You can also reach the beaches from Trebalúger. They never get crowded but you'll often see pleasure boats moored off the shore in summer.

25 BINIGAUS

39.9201, 4.0247

Binigaus exudes its own special energy. Just a few minutes' walk from the resort of Sant Tomàs, this beach with its ochre sands and crystal-clear waters is a particular favourite with tourists and locals. The hollows formed by the sea in the clay walls, which provide shade for bathers, are one of the attractions of this large beach which is narrow in places.

Please note: Although they may seem harmless, mud baths cause severe erosion so please bear this in mind when you visit the Cavalleria and Cala Pilar beaches.

THE BEST SUNSETS

There are so many places on Menorca where you can enjoy magical sunsets. In the north, or south, by the sea or inland, at a terrace or from a lighthouse, in Ciutadella or even Maó harbour... There are myriad possibilities on this island that seems to turn its face eastwards when the sun begins to set. Here are the best sunsets, the essential ones... but there are many more. Come along and see them!

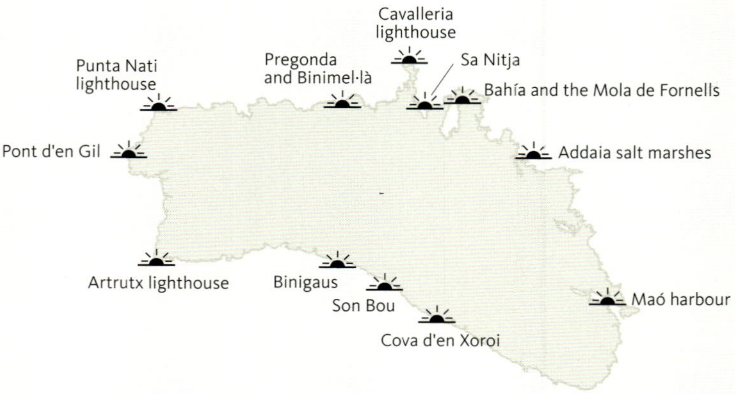

26 SON BOU

39.8990, 4.0709

Stretching for 2.5 kilometres, Son Bou is Menorca's longest beach. It has two distinct sections. The first, in the west, is completely unspoilt, has no services, hotels or houses and backs onto the wetland area of Prat de Son Bou. The second section is more built up and has all kinds of services for tourists along with two hotels at the back that overlook the beach. On the eastern tip, you can visit the remains of an early-Christian basilica dating from the 5th century. The water quality is excellent, as it is on the rest of the Menorcan coast.

Prat de Son Bou

Prat de Son Bou is the second most important wetland area on Menorca after Albufera des Grau. The lagoon is fed by water from the two streams that flow from the Es Bec and Son Boter ravines. It is a popular bird-watching site.

27 CALA EN PORTER

39.8700, 4.1322

The mouth of the Cala en Porter ravine has lush vegetation. The steep cliffs make this sea inlet into a coastal site of great beauty. It is similar to other coves and beaches in the south of the island, and has abundant plants at the back, limestone walls with fairly steep sides and a bank of fine, light-coloured sand which extends to the seabed. The beach stands at the foot of the resort of the same name where you'll find, inside a clifftop grotto, one of the most spectacular nightclubs in the Mediterranean: the Cova d'en Xoroi. It has been in business for five decades.

28 CALA DE BINIDALÍ

39.9155, 4.2866

A small beach with white sand and limpid waters at the mouth of the Binidalí ravine. It nestles at the end of a narrow cove which, like many others in the south of the island, is sheltered from the winds. A well-maintained stone path leads down to the beach. On the right-hand side there is a small house with a jetty which blends in perfectly with the landscape. You'll find these types of buildings all along the Menorcan coast. They were traditionally used as shelters by fishermen.

CALES COVES

Cales Coves is a natural landmark created by the sea which is well worth seeing from higher ground. It doesn't attract many bathers but boats moored off its shores are a common sight. The cliff walls above the beach contain the most important necropolis on the island.

29 CALA DE BINIBÈQUER

39.9155, 4.2866

This is one of the most popular beaches in the south of Menorca. The ease of access, tourist services – including a snack bar – and the pine glade at the back with a picnic area, are just some of the reasons why it has become a firm favourite with families. Although the beach is close to a busy resort, the scenery makes you feel you are in the middle of nature.

Bathing on the rocks

All along the coast of Sant Lluís there are purpose-made bathing areas on the rocks. You'll find some of the best ones in the resorts of Binibèquer Vell and Binissafúller, where Es Caló Fondo is one of the most popular. It is also well worth taking a dip from the small jetties in Biniancolla and Cala Torret.

Caló de Rafalet

It is hard to decide which is the best: the path through the lush ravine with its majestic forest of evergreen oaks; or the tiny, charming cove at the end. Whatever you decide, this is certainly a magical place that is well worth a visit. Just a short distance away, you'll find the resort of S'Algar, which offers all kinds of services.

30 PUNTA PRIMA

39.8133, 4.2809

Along with Binibèquer and Es Grau, this is one of the most popular beaches with families with young children due to the ease of access, services and excellent-quality waters. These aspects, together with the fact that it is part of a holiday resort with a large number of villas and hotels, account for the large number of bathers. You can see the Illa de l'Aire lighthouse in front of the beach.

There are countless green areas on Menorca, which was declared a Biosphere Reserve in 1993. Nowadays 66% of the island is protected and just 4.9% of its land mass has been built on. This is particularly remarkable if we bear in mind that we are talking about somewhere in the Mediterranean. Below you will find the essential sites that best represent "Menorca's green landscape".

EXPLORING MENORCA'S **GREEN LANDSCAPE**

- Sa Bassa Verda
- S'Albufera des Grau
- Binigaus ravine
- Favàritx
- Sanitja
- Algendar ravine
- Mongofre and Fornells salt marshes
- Pont d'en Gil
- Illa de l'Aire
- Marine reserve

1

Sa Bassa Verda

Ciutadella

Sa Bassa Verda, or green pond, is situated just a short distance away from the Algaiarens beaches, and is one of the most wonderful spots in the north of Menorca, particularly in the coldest months when it floods (the pond is fed only by rainwater). Together with 25 other ponds on the island, Sa Bassa Verda is part of a European Union project to preserve temporary ponds that are considered habitats of special interest due to their fragility, uniqueness and scarcity.

TOP 10 PLACES

2

S'Albufera des Grau

Maó

This is the most important wetland area on the island and forms the core of the Albufera des Grau Natural Park. The saltwater lagoon in the centre covers an area of 70 ha and is a refuge for many bird species, making it a great place for bird-watching. We recommend you visit the Rodríguez Femenías reception centre where you'll find an exhibition about the park and information about the three self-guided itineraries you can go on.

3

Binigaus ravine

Es Migjorn Gran

The south of the island is criss-crossed by 16 ravines: the longest are found in the centre of the Migjorn plateau. One of them is Binigaus, which emerges onto the beach of the same name and is a very interesting natural site. Along the route there are two places to bear in mind: the Cova des Coloms, a vast natural cave which was used as a shrine in prehistoric times or place of pilgrimage, and the Cova de na Polida.

TOP 10 PLACES

4

Favàritx

Maó

Favàritx is another of the wonderful treasures in the Albufera des Grau Natural Park. Its ancient rocky outcrops make it one of the island's most unique spots. The strata, comprising detrital rocks, sandstone and slate, date back 400 million years. This is one of the most interesting geological trails on the island.
For further information: www.geologiamenorca.org

5

Sanitja

Es Mercadal

The history, culture, landscape and natural scenery of Sanitja, on the Cavalleria peninsula, in the north of the island, make it a more than worthy contender for 'essential' status. This natural port, with its 18th-century defence tower in the east, the remains of a Roman settlement in the west, and the Cavalleria lighthouse in the north, is a little piece of heaven inside an environmentally protected area.

6

Algendar ravine

Ferreries

Stretching for nearly 7 km, this is the longest ravine on Menorca. It begins in Ferreries and ends at Cala Galdana. It is home to a wealth of fauna and flora, as well as archaeological treasures such as those found in the caves, the Cova Murada and Cova des Càrritx. It is also the most imposing ravine, with sides that are 80 m high in places. Two of its places of interest are found near the start, not far from Ferreries: the ancient path, the Camí Reial, and the Pas d'en Revull. This is certainly one of the island's natural gems.

7

Mongofre and Fornells salt marshes

Maó / Fornells

Menorca is also home to a series of environmentally significant coastal salt marshes: Addaia and Mongofre in the municipality of Maó, which are part of the Albufera des Grau Natural Park, and the Concepció salt flats in Fornells, which are used today for harvesting salt. They can both be reached along the bridle path, the Camí de Cavalls.

8

El Pont d'en Gil

Ciutadella

A spectacular natural arch sculpted by the sea out of a rocky promontory that juts out from the Cala en Blanes resort in Ciutadella. Located in an area of cliffs, near the magical Punta Nati, the Pont d'en Gil is one of the most picturesque sites on Menorca. It also conceals an extremely beautiful, 200-metre-long underground cave.

9

Illa de l'Aire

Sant Lluís

This is one of the most environmentally important small islands on Menorca. It is the habitat of the endemic black lizard, known as Lilford's wall lizard (*Podarcis lilfordi lilfordi*), as well as a stopover site for migratory birds. Plans are underway to turn the island into a marine reserve.

▸ p. **90**

10

Marine reserve

North coast of Menorca

"Menorca's green landscape" stretches beyond its coast, beaches and cliffs. The seabed around the island is another of its great natural attractions, particularly the area between the North Menorca Marine Reserve, which includes an area of 5,119 ha between Fornells and Cap Gros, in Ciutadella. It is well worth taking a dip in its waters to discover its rich biodiversity.

GOOD PRACTICE GUIDE

Show respect for nature

Respect the plants and animals, avoid damaging crops and walking over the dunes as they are a habitat for flora and fauna that are essential for the preservation of the beaches.

Do not leave a mess

Leave the paths as you found them. Take any litter away with you, including organic waste, and dispose of it in the bins provided. If you have a pet with you, remember to clean up after it.

Do not build stone stacks

Building stone stacks is harmful to the flora and fauna and defaces the landscape. Help us keep it in its natural state.

Close gates behind you

Gates divide up properties and plots of land and play an important role in farmers' everyday lives. If you leave them open, animals may escape so remember to close them behind you.

Look after the beaches

Cigarette ends are not biodegradable and can remain in the sand for up to five years, so take them away with you. If you take food or drink with you to the beach, use reusable containers and cutlery and avoid using glass. Use waterproof and biodegradable sunscreen. And show respect for other bathers and your surroundings by keeping the noise down.

Keep to the signposted paths

Avoid walking through fields as this might cause damage to the natural environment or private property.

Keep the noise down

Respect the peace and quiet of your surroundings.

Keep your speed down

You are on Menorca, so there's no need to hurry. Just enjoy the island's byways and scenery, whether you're in a car, on a boat or bike.

Respect private property

Do not trespass on private property. Ask for permission to enter first. Use public footpaths and rights of way.

A great memento

Make sure your memento of Menorca isn't a stone or sand from the beach. A beach is made up of individual grains of sand and each grain that disappears causes serious damage. So think twice before you pick something up from the ground as you might unwittingly be taking away a plant species in danger of extinction or an archaeological relic.

Free camping

Free camping is not allowed on Menorca. You can spend the night at the beach but you can't pitch a tent. If you like camping, find out about the campsites on the island.

Do not light fires

Avoid any risk of fire. Do not discard cigarette ends. Lighting fires is against the law.

Keep to the marker buoys

If you are on a boat, use the entry and exit channels to reach the shore. The marker buoys define the swimming and sailing areas.

Do not damage the Neptune grass

If you are going sailing, use the anchor buoys and avoid dropping anchor whenever possible. If you do so, choose areas where there is no Neptune grass growing as it makes a valuable contribution to creating sand and is vitally important in protecting the coast.

Avoid taking mud baths

Mud baths are becoming increasingly popular and are causing erosion at certain places on the coast as well as endangering the beach ecosystem. Please respect the environment and avoid this practice. Be aware that clay embankments do not regenerate.

Respect our landmarks

Archaeological remains are everybody's birthright. Do not climb on them as this will cause irreparable damage. If you want to paint or write, use a notepad.

Do not use metal detectors

And, of course, do not use metal detectors at archaeological sites or in those areas where a site is thought to exist. This practice is punishable by law.

Do not pick up any materials

Do not pick up stones or pieces of pottery from the ground. This could result in the loss of an important part of our history.

Do not disturb shipwreck sites

The remains of ancient shipwrecks are also important in carrying out research into our history and have the same protected status as archaeological sites. Treat them with respect.

MENORCA
RESERVA DE BIOSFERA

Menorca is a **BIOSPHERE RESERVE**
and we are concerned about its preservation.

A JOURNEY TO THE PAST

The vestiges of Menorca's prehistoric past are truly unique. This is due to a number of reasons: their type – the megalithic **taulas** and **navetas** are found nowhere else in the world –, their excellent state of repair, monumental scale, the building techniques used, and their density (there are more than 1,500 sites in an area of just 702 km^2, or, in other words, more than two per km^2). These are all reasons that support the bid to include Talayotic Menorca on the World Heritage list.

The island's prehistoric history is divided into five phases:

Dolmenic (2100 - 1600 BC)
Naviform (1600 - 1050 BC)
Proto-talayotic (1050 - 850 BC)
Talayotic (850 - 550 BC)
Post-talayotic (550 - 123 BC)

Talayotic Menorca Guide. The prehistory of the island

A unique publication that will take you on a 4,000-year journey back in time to find out how the first Menorcan settlers lived. It includes illustrations, fact sheets and maps.

ISBN 978-84-8478-6429

TOP 10 PLACES

Naveta des Tudons

Naviform-Talayotic

Me-1 road, 40 km marker post (Ciutadella)

This is the most iconic monument from talayotic culture because it is in such an excellent state of repair and is a unique type of tomb. The bones of 100 individuals were found inside. The name 'naveta' (small boat in Catalan) was coined because these structures resemble an upturned boat. There are two other navetas at the Rafal Rubí site in Alaior.

Trepucó

Naviform-Islamic period

Camí de Trepucó (Maó)

Covering an area of almost 5,000 m², Trepucó is one of the largest talayotic settlements on the island. Two of the four original talayots, a taula precinct, the remains of dwellings and a section of wall have been found inside its wide perimeter. There are signs that it may have been destroyed in the 2nd century BC, at the time of the 2nd Punic War.

Talatí de Dalt

Naviform-Islamic period

Me-1 road, 4 km marker post (Maó)

The settlement of Talatí de Dalt has some of the most representative structures of talayotic culture, including a talayot, a taula precinct, hypostyle chambers, dwellings and hypogeas. Its most outstanding feature is the taula with its leaning pilaster. The settlement was inhabited until the Islamic period.

Torre d'en Galmés

Naviform-Islamic period

Camí de Torre d'en Galmés (Alaior)

The Torre d'en Galmés settlement covers an area of 6.6 km^2, making it the largest on the Balearic Islands. It is also one of the most spectacular due to the density, diversity and good state of repair of its buildings and structures. It has three talayots, a taula precinct, hypogea and several dwellings, including the Cartailhac circle. It is the only site with an interpretation centre.

Torralba d'en Salord

Naviform-Islamic period

Road from Alaior to Cala en Porter, 3 km marker post (Alaior)

The monumental stone slab, or taula, standing 4 m high in the centre of this talayotic settlement makes Torralba d'en Salord a must-see. The site also has two talayots, hypostyle chambers, hypogea, artificial cave necropolises, water tanks and the remains of other buildings.

Torrellafuda and Torretrencada

Talayotic

Me-1 road, 36 km marker post (Ciutadella)

The talayotic settlements of Torrellafuda and Torretrencada stand just a short distance apart. They both contain characteristic features of talayotic culture, including taula precincts and talayots. The taula at Torretrencada is particularly noteworthy, with its pilaster attached to the back of the taula, as well as the remains of the wall at Torrellafuda.

Son Catlar

Talayotic-post-talayotic

Camí de Sant Joan de Missa (Ciutadella)

You can still see the remains of a high wall stretching for 900 m, with several bastions and talayots and a taula precinct, which account for its monumental scale. A group of researchers insist on the importance of Son Catlar between the 4th and 2nd centuries BC, a time of conflict in the Mediterranean due to the Punic Wars.

THE CAMÍ DE CAVALLS

The bridle path, the **Camí de Cavalls (GR-223)** opened to the public in 2010 and has become one of Menorca's great natural attractions. Its origins are unclear but it is thought to date back to the Middle Ages (14th century) when it was used as a defence point. The path covers the entire perimeter of the island and is 184 km long and divided into 20 stages. This makes it the perfect way to get to know this tiny Mediterranean haven in greater depth.

You can explore the path on foot, by bike (ATB) and on horseback. **But never with a motorised vehicle**.

Remember to take food and water with you, as well as a cap and sunscreen in the hottest months.

Please bear in mind the instructions in the **Good Practice Guide**.

▸ pp. **142-143**

The Camí de Cavalls

Discover every detail of one of the most fascinating natural trails in the Mediterranean. This guide features all the information you'll need to explore the different sections of the Camí de Cavalls and enjoy the experience to the full.

ISBN 978-84-8478-5057

GR-223

Camí de Cavalls

STAGES

1. **Maó ▸ Es Grau**
   DISTANCE **10 km** | DIFFICULTY **Moderate**
2. **Es Grau ▸ Cap de Favàritx**
   DISTANCE **8.8 km** | DIFFICULTY **Moderate**
3. **Cap de Favàritx ▸ Arenal d'en Castell**
   DISTANCE **13.6 km** | DIFFICULTY **Moderate**
4. **Arenal d'en Castell ▸ Cala Tirant**
   DISTANCE **10.8 km** | DIFFICULTY **Easy**
5. **Cala Tirant ▸ Binimel·là**
   DISTANCE **9.6 km** | DIFFICULTY **Moderate**
6. **Binimel·là ▸ Els Alocs**
   DISTANCE **8.9 km** | DIFFICULTY **Hard**
7. **Els Alocs ▸ Algaiarens**
   DISTANCE **9.7 km** | DIFFICULTY **Moderate**
8. **Algaiarens ▸ Cala Morell**
   DISTANCE **5.4 km** | DIFFICULTY **Easy**
9. **Cala Morell ▸ Punta Nati**
   DISTANCE **7.4 km** | DIFFICULTY **Easy**
10. **Punta Nati ▸ Ciutadella**
    DISTANCE **5 km** | DIFFICULTY **Easy**
11. **Ciutadella ▸ Cap d'Artrutx**
    DISTANCE **13.2 km** | DIFFICULTY **Easy**
12. **Cap d'Artrutx ▸ Cala en Turqueta**
    DISTANCE **13.3 km** | DIFFICULTY **Easy**
13. **Cala en Turqueta ▸ Cala Galdana**
    DISTANCE **6.4 km** | DIFFICULTY **Easy**
14. **Cala Galdana ▸ Sant Tomàs**
    DISTANCE **10.8 km** | DIFFICULTY **Moderate**
15. **Sant Tomàs ▸ Son Bou**
    DISTANCE **6.4 km** | DIFFICULTY **Easy**
16. **Son Bou ▸ Cala en Porter**
    DISTANCE **8 km** | DIFFICULTY **Moderate**
17. **Cala en Porter ▸ Binissafúller**
    DISTANCE **11.8 km** | DIFFICULTY **Easy**
18. **Binissafúller ▸ Punta Prima**
    DISTANCE **8.1 km** | DIFFICULTY **Easy**
19. **Punta Prima ▸ Cala Sant Esteve**
    DISTANCE **7.3 km** | DIFFICULTY **Easy**
20. **Cala Sant Esteve ▸ Maó**
    DISTANCE **6 km** | DIFFICULTY **Easy**

SIGHTSEEING BY BIKE AND ATB

Menorca is the perfect destination for sightseeing by bike. In addition to the **Camí de Cavalls**, the island has a 75-km cycling route, comprising seven signposted stages, as well as a great many inland and coastal cycle paths. The varied terrain and types of path, which include short steep climbs through the constantly changing landscape, are more than enough reasons to explore the island on two wheels.

The **Cycling Route** can be done in stages or in one day, provided you have access to public transport at your arrival point. Another option is to do it in stages and combine it with other cycle paths.

We recommend you use all-terrain bikes (ATB).

Remember to take food and water with you, as well as a cap and sunscreen in the hottest months.

Please bear in mind the instructions in the **Good Practice Guide.**

▸ pp. **142-143**

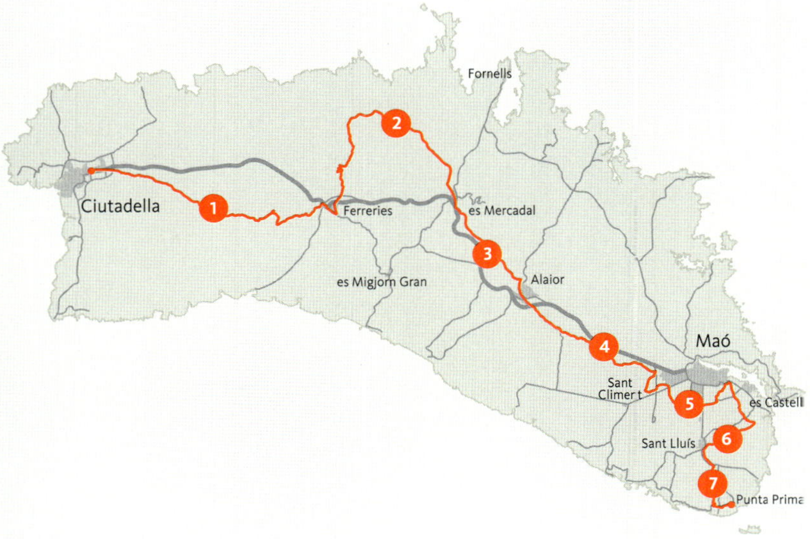

CYCLING ROUTE
Ciutadella ▸ Punta Prima
75 km | DIFFICULTY **Moderate**

1. **Ciutadella ▸ Ferreries**
DISTANCE **18.7 km** | DIFFICULTY **Moderate-Hard**
2. **Ferreries ▸ Es Mercadal**
DISTANCE **16 km** | DIFFICULTY **Hard**
3. **Es Mercadal ▸ Alaior**
DISTANCE **7.5 km** | DIFFICULTY **Easy**
4. **Alaior ▸ Maó**
DISTANCE **14.3 km** | DIFFICULTY **Easy**
5. **Maó ▸ Es Castell**
DISTANCE **7.2 km** | DIFFICULTY **Easy**
6. **Es Castell ▸ Sant Lluís**
DISTANCE **6.2 km** | DIFFICULTY **Easy**
7. **Sant Lluís ▸ Punta Prima**
DISTANCE **5.3 km** | DIFFICULTY **Easy**

Creativity, authenticity and quality are concepts that have always been inextricably linked to the products Made in Menorca, whether they're handcrafted or manufactured goods. Some of them have achieved worldwide renown and are particularly outstanding, such as mayonnaise, footwear – spearheaded by the *abarca* sandal –, and cheese. The list is extensive. Here are some of the essential ones.

MADE IN **MENORCA**

- Cheese
- Mayonnaise
- Wine
- Sausages and cured meats
- Pastries
- Cuisine
- Gin
- *Llaüt*
- Footwear
- Abarcas

1

Cheese

Menorcan cheese has been named one of the best cheeses in the world, and deservedly so. It has also won prizes at the World Cheese Awards. The intense flavour, salty tang, and square shape are the most characteristic features of one of the most historic products Made in Menorca (pottery fragments suggest cheese was first made on the island in prehistoric times). The cheeses are made from cow's milk and come in three types: mild, semi-mature and mature.

2

Mayonnaise

A great deal has been written about the origins of mayonnaise. It was originally associated with French cuisine but recent studies show that the most international of sauces originated on Menorca. It appears that the French imported it when they occupied the island (1756-1763) and the Duke of Richelieu, the nephew of the cardinal, is said to have introduced it to French cuisine and from there to the rest of the world.

3

Wine

Wine tastes of the land where it is produced. And Menorcan wines have a markedly Mediterranean, island flavour. They have the characteristic freshness of young, bold wines. Although Menorcan wine is relatively new on the scene there are documents that show the island was producing wine in medieval times. There are currently eleven vineyards and eight wineries that produce red and white wines.

4

Sausages and cured meats

Menorca has a long-standing tradition of making sausages. The *sobrassada* is Sicilian in origin and one of the most popular. However there are others, including, *carn-i-xulla*, *camallot* and *botifarró*, which are the perfect example of snout-to-tail eating.

5

Cuisine

Menorcan cuisine is totally Mediterranean and draws on the products of the land and sea. It consists of simple recipes and humble dishes dictated by hard times, and also observes the seasonality of foods. The star dish is certainly the lobster stew, *caldereta de langosta*. Sampling this delicacy has become a tourist experience in its own right. We also suggest you sample other traditional dishes, including the soup, *oliaigua*; oven-baked tomatoes and potatoes – *perol* – cooked with skate, and *arròs de la terra*, which, despite having the word rice in its title, is actually made with semolina. And, of course, we recommend you sample new Menorcan cuisine and discover the creativity and quality of our chefs.

6

Pastries

Menorca has a long-standing tradition of pastry making. Proof of this is the vast repertoire of sweet and savoury pastries that have been handed down from generation to generation. The most popular sweet treats are *amargos* biscuits; a type of biscotti, *carquinyols*; little pastries, *pastissets*; flat fritters, *crespells*; and the spiral pastries, *ensaimadas*, while the crescent-shaped *rubiols*; cheese curd and meat pies, *formatjades*; spicy sausage rolls, *flaons*; and the flatbreads, *coques*, which come with a variety of toppings, reign supreme among the savoury ones.

7

Gin

Gin Xoriguer is the oldest gin in Spain. Its origins can be traced back to the middle of the 19th century, and although this spirit has traditionally been linked with the United Kingdom, it is also becoming increasingly associated with the Dutch. It is produced in ancient copper stills using wine alcohol, juniper berries and a blend of herbs. The result is one of the most aromatic gins on the market.

During the summer festivals, the favourite drink is *pomada*, a combination of gin and lemonade.

8

Llaüt

The *llaüt* is a traditional Balearic boat and a true Menorcan icon. Its solid structure and stability have earned it great prestige in the world of sailing. Originally, the *mestres d'aixa* (master carpenters of the shore) built them by hand from locally sourced wood. Today, Menorcan boat builders have perfected these craft, aesthetically and in terms of functionality.

Wood is also used to manufacture another Made in Menorca product: the Menorcan chair, also known as the *Coca Rossa*.

9

Footwear

Menorcan footwear has carved out a name for itself in the world of fashion through the commitment to design and quality of leading brands such as Jaume Mascaró, Pretty Ballerinas, Pons Quintana and Homers. These manufacturers have taken the Made in Menorca label up a notch, making it a key player in high-end footwear for women. And its prestige keeps on growing.

10

Abarcas

Abarcas are worth a special mention in the footwear industry due to their unique design and resounding success around the world. Once worn by the rural population, these sandals have conquered the public at large, to such an extent that they are now considered the epitome of Mediterranean footwear. In recent years, manufacturers have gone beyond the traditional model, made of cowhide and with a rubber sole, and added new designs and materials. This, together with a powerful marketing strategy, have brought them great commercial success.

When you buy a pair of *abarcas* make sure they have the *Avarca de Menorca* quality label which guarantees they are 100% genuine and Made in Menorca.

ESSENTIAL MENORCA

Sant Lluís, Menorca
T +34 971 15 04 51
www.triangle.cat
#livingtriangle
#madeinmenorca

Concept and texts
M. José Ferri Vizcaíno

Graphic design and illustrations
David Martínez

Editorial director
Aina Pla

©Picture credits
Ricard Pla (11a, 13, 17, 31a, 38, 43b, 52c, 53c, 55c, 57a, 63d, 63e, 68, 69a, 70abc, 74b, 77c, 80b, 81a, 87b, 88a, 92b, 99b, 102, 105, 107a, 112, 124, 125a, 126, 128ab, 129b, 132a, 138a, 139a, 146ab) **Juanjo Pons** (2, 12b, 20b, 21a, 25, 28a, 36a, 43a, 46c, 47a, 50, 53a, 57b, 60ab, 61, 65a, 79a, 90, 91b, 92a, 93, 94b, 96, 97b, 99a, 103, 104b, 109, 122, 127b, 129a, 130, 134, 136b, 137, 140ac, 142a, 143b, 144, 149, 158a, 159b) **David Arquimbau** (8a, 9b, 18ab, 27ab, 29a, 30, 31bc, 34b, 36b, 37b, 43c, 44ab, 47b, 48a, 51a, 52ab, 56c, 58b, 59, 63a, 63c, 64, 65bc, 67b, 69b, 71a, 76b, 78ab, 79b, 82a, 83abc, 94a, 107b, 110, 111, 125b, 139b, 154b) **Biel Puig** (6, 10b, 12a, 14, 21b, 26, 37c, 47c, 49, 56b, 62b, 86, 88b, 89, 91a, 91c, 95, 100, 106, 113, 114, 115, 116, 117ab, 119, 121, 140b) **Joan Mercadal** (19a, 32, 33, 34a, 35a, 40, 42ab, 45b, 48c, 55a, 66, 77a, 81b, 97a, 120, 127a, 131, 132b, 136a, 145a, 148ab) **Laia Moreno** (19b, 20a, 29b, 41a, 54, 62a, 101, 104a, 141c) **Joan Colomer** (35b, 41b, 63b, 76a, 76c, 77b, 78c) **David Cardona** (8b, 9a, 10a, 11b, 45a, 48b, 53b, 58a, 71c, 72, 74ac, 75a, 80a, 87a, 138b, 143a, 145b, 147) **Kike Cardona** (16a, 150b, 151, 158b) **Oriol Aleu** (16b, 152, 155ab, 156abc, 157ab) **Jaume Serrat** (28b) **Aina Pla** (37a, 37d, 46ab, 56a,111) **Tolo Balaguer** (51b, 62c, 150a) **Centre Artesanal de Menorca** (55b) **Miki Pons** (57c, 98, 142b) **Lluis Bertran** (82b) **Pons Quintana** (159a) **Sergi Escandell** (141ab) **Made in menorca** (154a)

Filmsetting
David Martínez

Image management and photo retouching
Aina Pla, Germán Campos, Biel Puig, Oleguer Farriol

Translation
Mark Waudby

Printed in Barcelona by
Tallers gràfics Soler, 6-2018

Legal deposit: Me 496-2018
ISBN: 978-84-8478-823-2

Published with the support of

GOIB CONSELLERIA CULTURA, PARTICIPACIÓ I ESPORTS
illenc Institut d'Estudis Balèarics

CONSELL INSULAR DE MENORCA

MENORCA TALAIÒTICA
Candidata Patrimoni Mundial

CHARACTER DESIGN QUARTERLY

Image © Kelsey Buzzell

CONTENTS

04
BEHIND THE COVER ART: TOM BOOTH
Admire Tom's enchanting artwork and tumultuous creative journey

18
STORY LINES
Federico Etchegaray explains the importance of great linework

22
THE BASHFUL AVIATOR
Isaac Jadraque follows our random five-word brief to craft an unusual character

36
CHARACTERIZE THIS
Corah Louise designs an effective "unimpressed mushroom"

38
MEET THE ARTIST: HAIMENG CAO
Haimeng offers a look into his varied design practice creating sci-fi worlds

48
STORYTELLING THROUGH GESTURE
Samantha Vilfort teaches how to tell a character's story through emotive gesture

52
MEET THE ARTIST: KELSEY BUZZELL
With a background in architecture and interior design, illustrator Kelsey has much to share

WELCOME TO *CHARACTER DESIGN QUARTERLY 10*

Gracing this issue's cover is the captivating art of acclaimed illustrator Tom Booth. A master of storytelling, Tom has employed a variety of design tools to create an emotionally charged scene with a compelling narrative that leaves you wanting to find out more. Read Tom's interview to discover the man behind the art.

Additionally, you have the opportunity to delve into the personal sketchbook of Senior UI Artist at Insomniac Games, Jose Ciceraro, and uncover the workings of his fascinating creative mind. Featuring interviews with illustrator, Kelsey Buzzell, and concept artist, Haimeng Cao, we present a banquet of art styles and diverse insights into the character design and world-building industries. Furthermore, Ioana Sopov offers a redesign of the classic "evil queen"; creating a character with ferocious attitude and a contemporary palette.

As character design at its core is about crafting a new life, our *Characterize This* feature asks artists to bring an otherwise inanimate object to life; with its own past, present, and future. Corah Louise crafted an unimpressed mushroom, with its own set of irritants and poisonous personality. This playful mini-feature reminds us that it's important to stay loose and allow time for fun explorative work. So, if you're feeling creatively blocked, why not try animating something you can see around you right now, and let your imagination run wild!

SOPHIE SYMES
EDITOR

Image © Ioana Sopov

66
GALLERY
Helen Bucher, Janice Sung, and Marie Gräbener share their art with us

74
HOW TO KEEP A SKETCHBOOK
Discover how Jose Cicero uses his sketchbooks to contain his initial ideas

84
HOW I STYLIZE
Erica Hodne demonstrates how she stylizes her unique characters

90
REDESIGNING CLASSIC CHARACTERS
Ioana Sopov gives the classic "evil queen" archetype a contemporary makeover

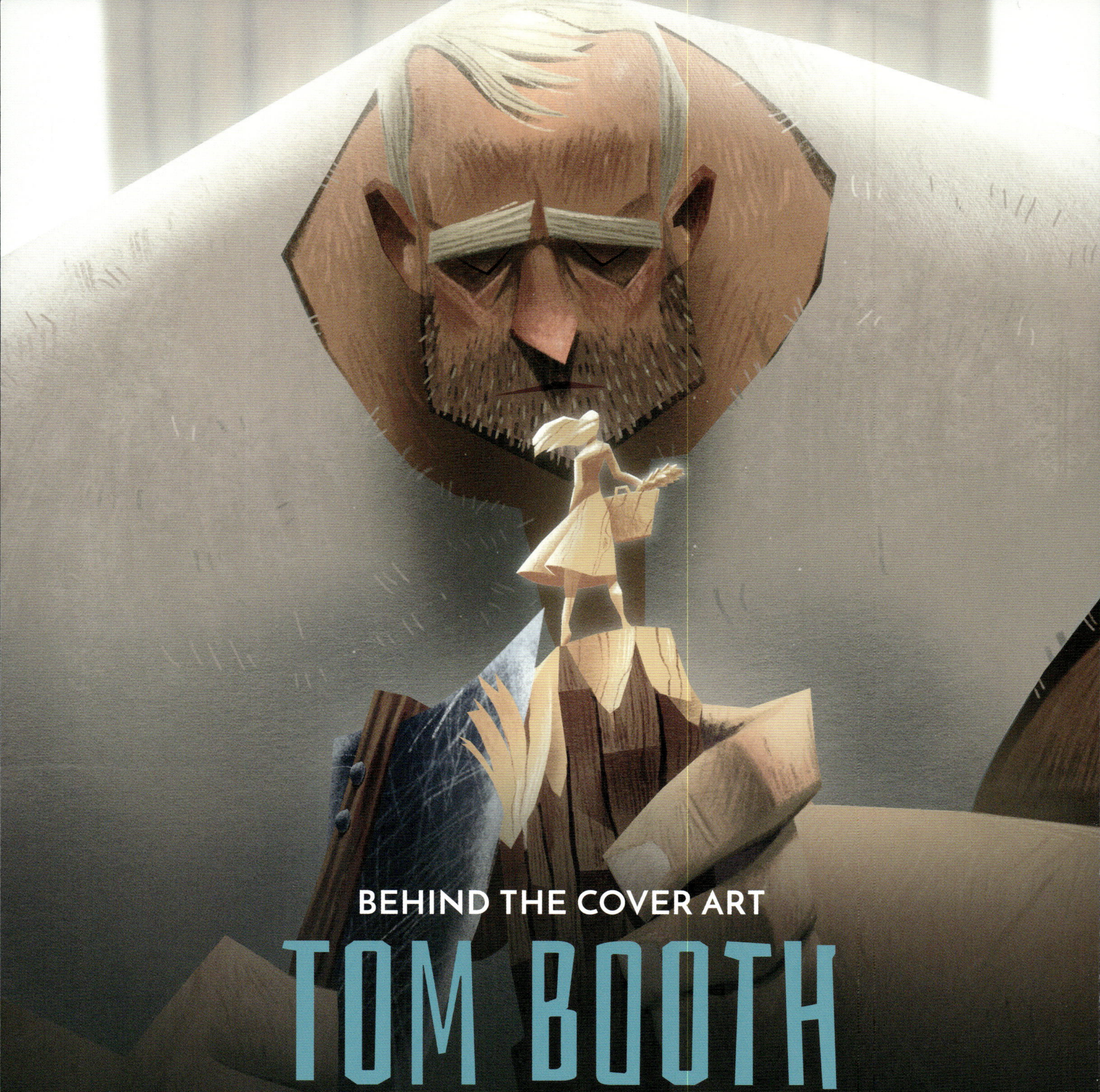

BEHIND THE COVER ART

TOM BOOTH

Art director by day, children's author and illustrator by night, storyteller and critically acclaimed artist Tom Booth is the talent behind this issue's stunning cover art. With a passion for storytelling, whether through words or pictures, he's no stranger to hard work, patience, and taking risks in order to develop his craft. While career highs include working with the captain of the New York Yankees on his first children's book, Tom has also learned to value the perspective and renewed focus that only comes through disappointment and failure. We talked to Tom about his varied career, the importance of storytelling, the transience of failure, and the process behind his moving cover illustration.

Hi Tom, thank you for creating such an engaging and emotionally charged cover for us! For those who aren't familiar with your work, could you please tell us about your career so far?

For the past ten years I've divided my time between the publishing and animation industries, most recently working as an art director and production artist by day, and authoring and/or illustrating picture books, middle grade novels, and my own stories at night. I first got into publishing after a brief stint at Nicktoons, which was my first job after graduating from college. I leaned towards picture books because I love how the text and art play off each other, as well as the challenge of fitting a story into what can often seem like a relatively limited format.

"SUCCESS IS NEVER FINAL AND FAILURE ISN'T FATAL"

I was lucky enough to get an agent after college and had plans to publish a graphic novel. However, I still had so much to learn about publishing and taking on a graphic novel with such limited experience was more challenging than I anticipated. With nothing to sell, my agent and I agreed to part ways, and I was convinced I would probably never get published. Fortunately, the low point came with some perspective; success is never final and failure isn't fatal. It's part of a favorite quote of mine that is often attributed to Winston Churchill, although I'm not certain if he's the one who coined it: "Success is not final; failure is not fatal. It is the courage to continue that counts." The quote refers to how we respond to challenges in life. I regrouped, focused on my weaknesses, and moved on to make new connections and new stories that led to my breakthrough in publishing: illustrating a picture book for Yankees' captain, Derek Jeter, as well as selling my author debut.

Working in a creative field has some unique challenges, one of which is putting your ideas and work out into the world. Sometimes your work finds an audience that showers you with praise, but sometimes that audience can turn on you. Regardless of the outcome, it is important to push yourself to produce new work. In my experience, the work you produce when you've been hit the hardest can be the work that is the most honest and impactful.

This page: *Purple Bear* – A concept sketch for a children's book

This spread: *Dragon* – Characters from a children's book idea I'm developing

How do you find the balance working full-time as Art Director at Scholastic and as a freelance artist in your spare time?

Finding the balance can be tricky at times. Working as an art director, I have the benefit of being inspired by my team and working with them to meet a variety of challenges presented by our clients. Working as an author/illustrator and concept artist is similar, in that I can rely on my editors and art directors to help envision a story or character, but it's also more solitary for most of the production process. I enjoy both styles of work, but I also reserve time and energy to explore personal projects in which I'm able to take more risks and develop as a storyteller.

The desire to become an effective storyteller seems to be prevalent among illustrators. Why do you think that is?

We are all storytellers. Whether you tell your story with words or pictures, storytelling helps us comprehend and share our experiences with others. I started to draw to put ideas to paper, and to record and respond to the world around me. Similar to writing in a journal, illustration is my way of interpreting the world. Even if an illustration is depicting a character with purple skin on a faraway, fantasy planet, I'm drawing from my own experiences to inform that character's appearance and personality, and the audience can pick up on that. The better you are at telling your story – which only comes with lots of practice and patience – the stronger the connection is between you, your work, and your audience.

You've had such an exciting and varied career – of all the projects you've worked on over the years, which did you enjoy the most?

It's hard to beat the feeling you get from publishing your first book, especially when it involves working with people you admire. My first book as an illustrator, *Derek Jeter Presents Night at the Stadium*, required that I visit Yankee Stadium for reference and spend some time with the team in their clubhouse before they played the Mets. A few months prior I'd convinced myself that I'd never be published, so suddenly working with the captain of the Yankees on his first children's book was quite a shock. Fortunately I'd learned to step up to the proverbial plate from my prior attempts to publish work.

It's fantastic that you visit schools and libraries to share your work. What made you want to do this?

As an author and illustrator of picture books, it's common for publishers, book stores, and schools to set up events for you to talk to kids about your journey and work. Kids aren't shy about sharing their opinions and I've had more humbling moments than I can count when kids let me know if a story or sketch needs work. But I've also had the good fortune to see kids respond to my work and learn from my drawing lessons. I think kids can sometimes be discouraged from drawing when they realize the career that could follow isn't as linear or clear-cut as others. But I think the skill of drawing is invaluable in such a visually focused world. My hope is that visiting schools and working with kids will teach them the value in being able to find their creative voice and express their own ideas.

Children can be so brutally honest! Have you had any particularly entertaining, or crushing feedback from children?

On the last stop of my first book tour, I opened by reading my new book to a room full of three to six year old kids. Everything was going well until a girl on the far left stood up and said, "I don't know if I have time for all of this." Apparently this particular four-year-old had a very busy schedule and I was in danger of encroaching on her next appointment. As I continued to read at a slightly faster pace, she interrupted two more times to remind me that she didn't have a lot of time. I followed the reading with a drawing tutorial and a brief Q&A, and as I was packing up to leave, I noticed that everyone had left but the little girl and her mom. It turned out the little girl had overheard her mom using that phrase earlier in the day and decided to try it out during my event. Months later, I got a letter from the girl's mom saying that her daughter had lost my book when they'd moved house. I sent her a new book with a little note and received multiple thank you cards. It's easy to forget that what can seem like negative feedback often comes from someone who is already a fan of what you do.

"IT'S EASY TO FORGET THAT WHAT CAN SEEM LIKE NEGATIVE FEEDBACK OFTEN COMES FROM SOMEONE WHO IS ALREADY A FAN OF WHAT YOU DO"

This spread: Characters from a children's book idea I'm currently developing based on emotion

Your books *Don't Blink!* and *Don't Tell!* offer an interactive element to young readers and have received great praise. What gave you the idea to create books that speak directly to the reader?

After I dusted myself off from failing to publish a graphic novel, I dove headfirst into picture books. I had a lot of ideas, but I couldn't really find any that worked – they were either too complex, too long, or too short, or not age-appropriate for such a young audience. One night, after failing yet again to come up with a story I liked, I decided instead to simply draw for fun. I was exhausted, blinking a lot, and had a funny thought: I could never beat one of my drawings in a staring contest. I realized that I'd never seen a picture book in which the characters and the reader have a staring contest, so I got to work. Within a few days – after a year of struggling to realize an idea – I suddenly found myself in a room full of people eager to develop my story and characters into a series.

This spread: Explorative work for a personal project based on the life of a woodsman

"I CAN'T IMAGINE DOING WHAT I DO WITHOUT SOME ELEMENT OF PLAY"

It's amazing that all it seemed to take was one unusual, out-of-the-blue idea and you were on to something successful. Do you think that these moments of play and experimentation are important to your design process?

I can't imagine doing what I do without some element of play. Most people probably call it "trial and error", but at the end of the day you're exploring, failing, falling, and getting back up to do it all over again. At some point in that process you lose track of what looks right and what doesn't, you make mistakes, and you loosen up. It's in that moment that I often find new ideas and new ways of looking at something I thought I knew. That said, those moments of play and discovery rarely come spontaneously. You still need to put down a lot of lackluster ideas before you find one that really stands out.

This spread: The final cover art image, created just for *CDQ 10*

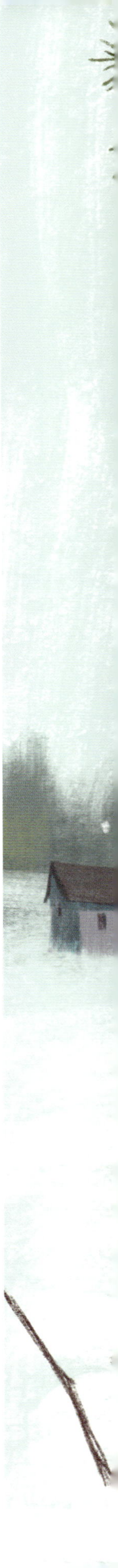

Your recent work has been filled with emotion and interlaced with narrative, with the occasional edge of darkness. Do you think your work is now beginning to lean towards an older audience?

My most recent work isn't necessarily inappropriate for kids, but it does explore heavier topics. The first image of my woodworker was created as a therapeutic exercise to help me process a difficult period in my life. I'd never intended to share it out of concern that it might disinterest my audience, which up until that point had come to expect mostly positive work from me. However, I was overwhelmed to find that the majority of my audience empathized with the feeling and thought behind the image. It's odd to feel excited about sharing an emotional and somewhat personal story, but the support of my followers has encouraged me not to shy away from exploring more difficult subject matter, especially if they have the potential to improve the personal growth of both myself and anyone else who chooses to experience the story.

This spread: First illustrations of the woodsman concept, created in Procreate on the iPad Pro

TOM BOOTH

"I'M CONSTANTLY ASKING MYSELF WHAT FEEDS THE STORY; THEN I GO ABOUT REMOVING ALL DISTRACTIONS"

This spread: Exploring perspectives with the woodsman concept. Created in Procreate on the iPad Pro

The viewing angles of your most recent work are so dynamic and engaging. How do you approach composition as a storytelling tool? And how do you decide where to set the viewing angle of a design?

Ultimately, my focus is on storytelling. With each illustration, I'm constantly asking myself what feeds the story; then I go about removing all distractions. For the cover, I wanted to keep the focus on the drawing of the woman, hoping that the viewer's eye would then travel to the shadow, and ultimately the character actually present in the scene. I thought a lot about what it would feel like to experience that moment from the character's perspective. I settled on a warrior who encounters an open, snowy canvas and uses a weapon to remember his life with his beloved. Having the drawing of her hand line up with the shadow of his, and the broken heart-shaped rock positioned at his shadow's heart, are meant to help feed the story, without feeling unnecessary. If received as intended, the image tells you about a moment, and a bit about the characters, while preserving enough mystery to make the viewer turn the page.

STORY LINES

FEDERICO ETCHEGARAY

In my opinion, character design is all about effective visual storytelling. The purpose of every element of the design is to give us information about who this character is. When great character design is achieved, anybody should be able to instantly get a good idea of what the character is feeling, and understand a bit about them.

Designers have a myriad of tools at their disposal and their ultimate success depends on how they use them. When I approach a new design, I first focus on the most important aspects of the character, getting to know who they are and what they are going through emotionally in the story. Once I know these answers, my mission becomes to reflect them through the design. I research the time in history they live in, environment they inhabit, culture they are part of, jobs they do, clothes they wear, and props they relate to. All of these elements inform the design choices and will help ground the character in reality and not in stereotypes.

When I start designing, I think in storytelling layers. These layers need to align with the main storyline and the character that is already defined in the screenplay. I first consider ethnicity; this will determine the facial structure and/or body structure, and I mix it with any specific character traits that might affect their face or body.

The next layer involves the dressing of the character. Physique and facial shapes are great tools to show character, but they are limited by the fact that we are born with them and they are not customizable. Dressing on the other hand is our choice and choice is what makes us unique, so they say a lot about who the character is and their personality. And on top of that they constantly change as times change and as we change – they are a storytelling goldmine!

THE COUNT

The count needs no introduction. To design him I study bats in hopes of finding new shapes or ideas for designing a vampire. From bats I take the huge ears and the elongated limbs and fingers you see here. I play with triangular shapes in the nose, jaw, and torso, but push proportions to keep the design fresh.

THE TELEPHONE OPERATOR

Even though she is just supposed to connect callers, this telephone operator can't help but pry on others people's conversations in search of some juicy gossip. For this piece I focus on the idea that even though operators used to hide unseen behind telephone lines, they cared a lot about their image, so I design an attractive woman wearing a nice dress, a trendy haircut and makeup, to reflect her vanity.

EL GAUCHO

Gauchos are the Uruguayan equivalent of the cowboy. They ride horseback, are followed by their loyal dogs, herd cattle, and play the Spanish guitar. For this design to communicate the character, it is really important to nail the traditional "gaucho" clothing; scruffy hairstyle and strong jaw, high cheekbones facial structure. To complete the character, I reflect the melancholic quality of gauchos in his facial expression.

"THROUGH POSING AND EXPRESSION, WE CAN RELATE TO CHARACTERS AND THEIR STORIES"

Props can also be used to relate deeply to who our character is; for example, a musician's guitar, or a skater's skateboard. Without them they wouldn't be who they are. These props usually tell us a lot about the characters' jobs, passions, or interests, and they can inform clothing or physical traits. A skater wears specific clothes and probably has scars or broken limbs from falling often.

Last but not least comes the posing and expression of the character. These two are the most important storytelling devices. Through posing and expression, we can relate to characters and their stories.

Using just linework, I have crafted six readable characters that tell us who they are, using all of these elements. So, no matter which style you choose to draw, either your own or someone else's, your success depends on the story your design tells, not the style.

THE PROSPECTOR

I wanted this gold rush prospector to have the face of someone who's been searching for gold for years, to no avail. He has tired eyes and a drawn face behind a long growing beard. The shape language of the pickaxe, slender wavy body, and the iconic hat tell the story of this wizened character.

THE EXPLORER

The classic British explorer smoking his pipe like a detective. Stylish hair, a strong jaw, and wonderful moustache make up his strong, inquisitive face. I draw his body blocky and square, to reflect the utilitarian form of his huge backpack, and push the overall silhouette to create clear negative space for his formal gentleman's pose.

THE OLIGARCH

This character is the Russian boss of bosses and as such he is larger than life, with a huge heavy-weight body that he carries with the help of a cane. I design his face similar to that of a big bullfrog, with sharp and menacing pointy ears and nose. And to finish his conniving face, I add a big mouth for spitting his huge lies and wild eyebrows to accentuate those evil eyes. He wears business clothes and has rings that reflect his wealth and power.

THE BASHFUL AVIATOR

ISAAC JADRAQUE

From a young age we have the ability to imagine and create new characters and worlds in which to tell their stories. As the years go by, many people forget this, or simply don't make the time for it in their lives. I think this is a big mistake. In this tutorial I will walk you through my creative process as I combine five random words (cat, pilot, bashful, carrot, and pink) into one character. You don't have to follow all of the steps, nor do them in the same order. I will be using Procreate for some sketches, then Photoshop for the rest of the process.

CHARACTER: CAT
OCCUPATION: PILOT
EMOTION: BASHFUL
OBJECT: CARROT
COLOR: PINK

DON'T STOP TO THINK, JUST DRAW

When you begin a project, whether personal or professional, the most important thing is to let loose and start drawing before you look at any references. In this case, the first thing that came to mind was the similarity between a carrot and a classic airplane. Instead of settling on the obvious form, I put wings on the carrot to make it fly, as if on some fantastic adventure. It also made me consider, is the carrot giant or the cat tiny? I liked the idea of a kitten that dreams of flying and plays with anything that looks like an airplane.

This page: In this early stage, let yourself go and start drawing no matter the main idea

IDEAS TRASH CAN

In the early stages I considered the possibility of making the carrot the character's vehicle. As the word "pilot" also appears in the brief, I could have made the character a pilot of airplanes, cars, or motorcycles. This would have been a very original and imaginative exercise in how to use leaves, roots, or other elements of nature to turn the carrot into a means of transport. However, I decided this would have reduced the role of the character, so I opted to add it as a toy instead. Don't dismiss an idea, however crazy it may seem. Consider it before discarding it definitively.

MIND MAP

Although it's not always necessary to do this step, it can prove very useful when you have to combine several concepts. It will help you work out which ideas you want to highlight more than others, and how they can work together and complement each other. While this time our brief clearly states that our character is a real life animal, a cat, at other times you may be able to map out and experiment with more ideas, including aliens and monsters. Don't dismiss any of your ideas, however outlandish they seem. You may change your mind when you look back at them later.

"DON'T DISMISS ANY OF YOUR IDEAS, HOWEVER OUTLANDISH THEY SEEM. YOU MAY CHANGE YOUR MIND WHEN YOU LOOK BACK AT THEM LATER"

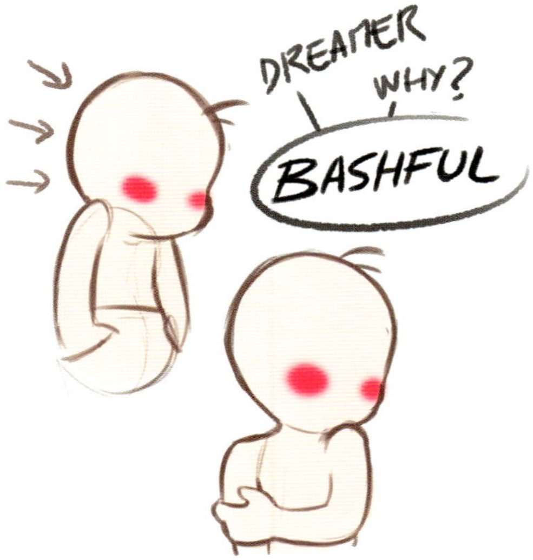

This page: Map out your ideas and explore how the concepts could work together

Opposite page: Explore as many versions as you can, but only share the ones that convince you

REFERENCES

Today we're fortunate enough to have an abundance of information at our fingertips via the internet. It's amazing how you can look up any word and see how the majority of people have the same visual reference for certain concepts, either from our collective imagination or from customs and traditions. Use it to help you communicate ideas everyone can understand. Or conversely, try to break free of the norm and look for new ways of illustrating the same idea in an original way. If you don't have a definite style, or if you're having to adapt to a different style, look for references from other artists.

EXPLORE

How many versions should you sketch out? Sometimes you will have a very clear idea for your character and will go with the first one you try. Sometimes we can fall in love with a pose, gesture, or design, which we cling to even if it doesn't fit the character. Whether it's for a client or for a personal project, always try to sketch out several versions. Don't settle for the first drawing. Explore other options, even if only to know that the first was the most convincing. And don't forget to number them to avoid mistakes and make it easier for the client to let you know which they've chosen.

GESTURAL LANGUAGE AND ATTITUDE

Once you've picked the winning sketch, you can start working on pose and attitude. I incorporated this into the previous step, so already have my chosen pose more or less clear. Most feelings and emotions have poses that people recognize and understand. Don't try to reinvent the wheel; most of our gestures and reactions are unconscious and are the product of instinct and evolution. For example, if you're afraid, you shrink, but if you feel brave, you stand tall and raise your chest. A bashful character should be seen to shy away, so in my sketches there is no element that stands out too much, except for the scarf.

"MOST FEELINGS AND EMOTIONS HAVE POSES THAT PEOPLE RECOGNIZE AND UNDERSTAND"

CONSTRUCTION

When clothes and accessories cover up most of a character's anatomy and body shape, we can be tempted to skip over this step. But even if you're well-skilled at drawing and have a lot of anatomical knowledge, there will still be errors to correct and more complicated parts that require further work. In this case, the character's legs had a slightly weird inward turn, so stripping it back helped me to visualize the pose as clearly as possible. If the character is for animation then remember that someone will have to move it, and therefore you need to know how its anatomy works, even if your style of drawing is very cartoon-like.

Above: Look for a pose that best represents the personality of the character

Left: If you have doubts about how any part of the body works, look for references

Opposite page: Only add elements that contribute something to the character

ADDING OR REMOVING PROPS

If your character has characteristic clothing or a distinguishable element that could catch the viewer's attention, try to highlight this as much as possible. Eliminate other elements that don't contribute to the image you're trying to convey with the character. I don't particularly like characters which are saturated with elements. Instead, I prefer to include only the essentials to create a stronger and more harmonious image. I knew I wanted the scarf to be the main element with this character, as it's the most dynamic of the props and stood out on the silhouette. I decided to remove the goggles, however, as these were very heavy and spoiled the silhouette.

"I PREFER TO INCLUDE ONLY THE ESSENTIALS TO CREATE A STRONGER AND MORE HARMONIOUS IMAGE"

ADD RHYTHM

This is something you must continue to work on as you build the character. Look at the internal structure of the character and how the lines play with each other. Avoid parallel lines unless absolutely necessary, or if you're following a pattern; for example, the lines of a shirt. Experiment as much as possible, comparing the straight lines against the curves. Force the drawing to the limits your character's anatomy allows; sometimes you can afford to break the rules of nature in pursuit of a better design.

"SOMETIMES YOU CAN AFFORD TO BREAK THE RULES OF NATURE IN PURSUIT OF A BETTER DESIGN"

THE PERFECT SILHOUETTE

Readjust any areas of the design that detract from your character having a recognizable silhouette. We're haunted by the image of a perfect silhouette in the media. Your character's silhouette doesn't necessarily need to be harmonious or have perfect measurements, but it does need to be easily identifiable. Eliminate small elements and details that only add noise to the character's silhouette, such as small wrinkles and creases.

Above: Study the shape language of the construction and force the pose to highlight its line of action

Left: The silhouette is one of the most important parts of a character's design

Opposite page: Linework is a crucial aspect in determining your drawing style

"BE CAREFUL THAT YOUR DRAWING DOESN'T LOSE ITS ORIGINALITY AND DYNAMISM"

LINEWORK

Now it's time to clean up your linework. Unless you're adapting to a certain style your client has requested, draw the line in the style you feel most comfortable with. But be careful that your drawing doesn't lose its originality and dynamism. If you're not going to color your drawing, try to provide all the information you can about volume and use different line thicknesses to illustrate variation. Beware of wrinkles, especially in the face. Unless our character is elderly, use very thin lines for this area. The same goes for clothes, unless they're meant to be ornate.

EXPRESSION SHEET

Sometimes it helps to accompany your character design with a sheet of expressions, even if your client hasn't asked for it or you don't have to prepare to animate it until later. Draw the expressions you think are necessary to complete your character. You don't have to do many; just include the extremes, plus any you think will help to define their attitude and character. If you have doubts, start by doing the squash and the stretch to see how the facial anatomy of your character works; which parts are rigid and which are more elastic.

"SOMETIMES IT HELPS TO ACCOMPANY YOUR CHARACTER DESIGN WITH A SHEET OF EXPRESSIONS, EVEN IF YOUR CLIENT HASN'T ASKED FOR IT"

This page: Choose expressions that best show the personality of your character

Opposite page: Look for color combinations that enhance your character's personality

"LOOK FOR COLOR COMBINATIONS AND TONES THAT FIT WITH YOUR CHARACTER'S ATTITUDE"

EXPLORING COLORS

Color can really help to enhance your drawing, as well as highlighting it visually. There is a strong relationship between color and the unconscious feelings they produce in us. Sometimes color can distract our attention from the important elements of a design. Look for color combinations and tones that fit with your character's attitude. Use bright colors if their personality is very dynamic, or if you want to highlight parts of the design; for example, the use of a vivid pink to show the character's flushed cheeks. Although the rest of the character's fur is also pink, it is mostly covered by clothing, making the cheeks stand out.

REMOVE COLOR!

Once you have chosen a color combination, try to pass it to grayscale. You'll see how the values work with each other and how they sit side by side. I wanted to highlight the cat's scarf so it stood out, but realized that the lapel of the windbreaker distracted from it. To fix this, I changed the lapel to a darker color in the next version. Try and ensure your drawing has an adequate balance of black and white (unless your character wears a set uniform/outfit like the Pope or Darth Vader) and play with the grayscale to get the intermediate volume.

This page: This step will help you to see which colors stand out from others

Opposite page: Don't distract with unnecessary details; it's better if some elements are suggested

ALMOST THERE...

Once you have your drawing in grayscale, start adding color masks. First add the midtones and shadows, lightly to begin with, then gradually increase the contrasts and accentuate the volumes. Your choice of brush will depend on the style of the design, but it's always better to use organic brushes with some texture to avoid the airbrush effect. You should also try and steer clear of the extreme and flat gradients characteristic of Photoshop. You can change the brush if necessary to simulate textures, such as hair or fabric, but try not to divert attention. In the next step we will add the light and make any last adjustments.

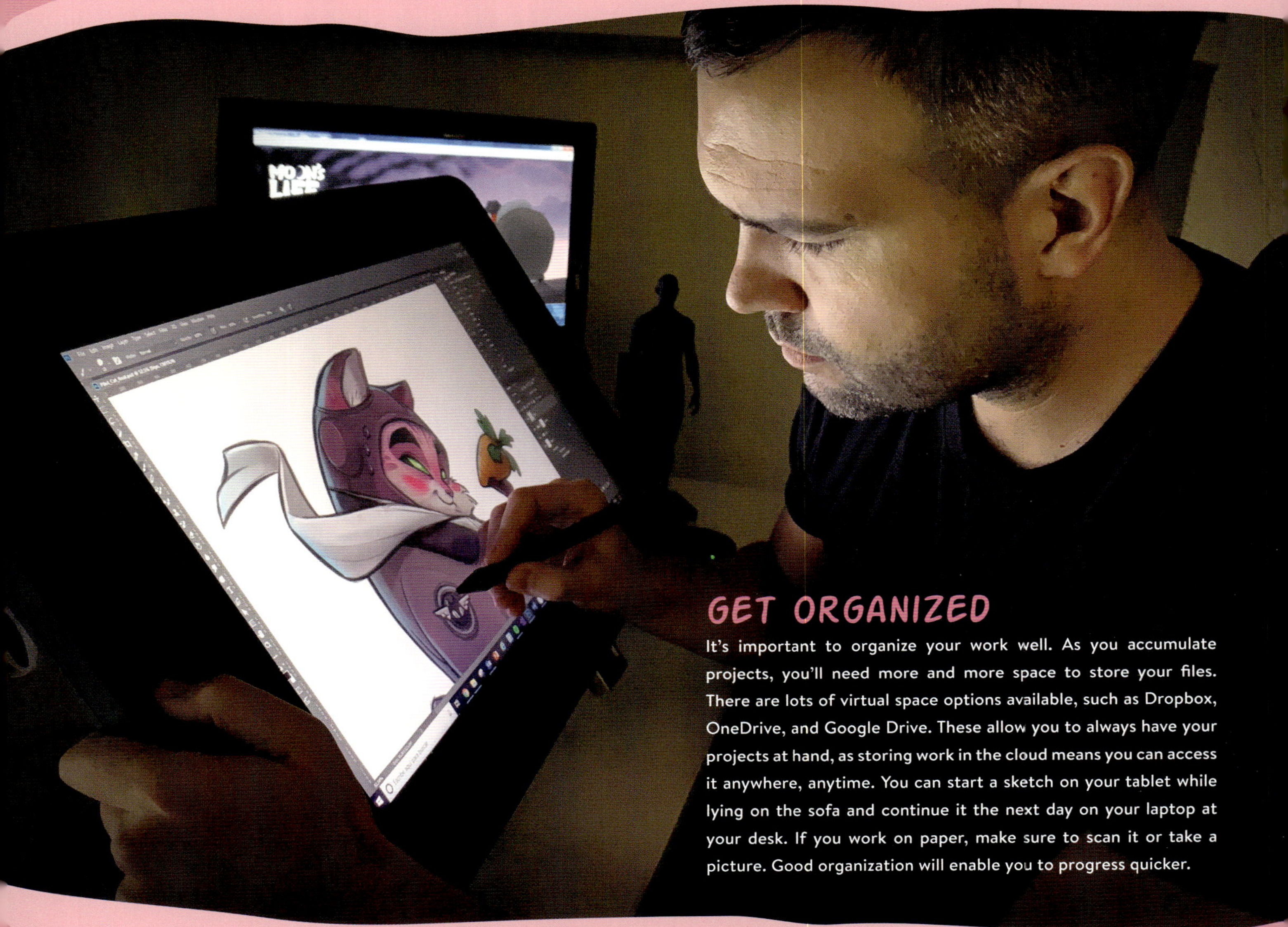

GET ORGANIZED

It's important to organize your work well. As you accumulate projects, you'll need more and more space to store your files. There are lots of virtual space options available, such as Dropbox, OneDrive, and Google Drive. These allow you to always have your projects at hand, as storing work in the cloud means you can access it anywhere, anytime. You can start a sketch on your tablet while lying on the sofa and continue it the next day on your laptop at your desk. If you work on paper, make sure to scan it or take a picture. Good organization will enable you to progress quicker.

FINAL ADJUSTMENTS

Although most of the time we may give the previous version to our client so they can feedback on the colors of the character, this final stage is where we can enhance our design a step further to give it that extra something. This includes light, textures, and effects. But be careful; if you spend too much time adding effects it can ruin your design and lose its freshness. Simply add a backlight to highlight some volumes, plus some noise and glazes of color to make it more attractive. And finally, don't forget to add a shadow to give weight to your drawing.

"IF YOU SPEND TOO MUCH TIME ADDING EFFECTS IT CAN RUIN YOUR DESIGN AND LOSE ITS FRESHNESS"

Opposite page: Only add the details necessary to improve your design

This page: Final image

CHARACTERIZE THIS: UNIMPRESSED MUSHROOM

CORAH LOUISE

Tasked with the brief to create an unimpressed mushroom character, I discuss my thought processes and design techniques, and demonstrate how to tackle imbuing character and emotion in otherwise inanimate objects.

From using references, to shape and color, I hope to help inspire your own unique character designs!

RESEARCH!

I begin with research. It may sound boring, but it is very important. There is nothing more inspiring than what already exists and so my first task is to take notes on shapes and colors while searching through pictures of mushrooms, and this is how I found the "Destroying Angel" mushroom.

The "Destroying Angel's" name, aesthetic and dangerous reality (being very poisonous) was a juxtaposition that immediately inspired a character! Combining the angelic paleness with a darker personality makes for a sinister profile. So, don't be fooled by this character, as she may seem beautiful but one step closer and she'll definitely bite!

IDENTIFY CHARACTERISTICS

I make a list of the key features of this deadly mushroom that I want the character to have – a long stem, a large mushroom head, and pale color. I use the long stem to play the neck, exaggerating the length and carrying this technique throughout the character.

SHAPE LANGUAGE

As my character has an easily aggravated and unapproachable personality, I use her shape language to show this. Triangular shapes and sharp edges are perfect for portraying a mysterious or feared character. I use these in the face with the nose and eyes, but also in the arms and mushroom cap.

WHY SO UNIMPRESSED?

I want to give her something to be unimpressed about – and mushrooms being out in nature offers the perfect setting for small animals to be a nuisance. I cross the arms, narrow the eyes, and draw her turning away from the viewer to give the over-the-shoulder-annoyed-glare.

"YOU NEED THEM TO TELL THE STORY BEFORE THEY EVEN SPEAK!"

THE DESTROYING ANGEL

And she is complete! My unimpressed mushroom is ready to impress! From reference to character, this challenge was so enjoyable! It is so important to take conscious decisions when designing a character, you need them to tell the story before they even speak! Each element of your design is important in expressing the character's personality to the audience – think color and shapes, and how you can play with the connotations. Make sure accessories add to the story and pose them with purpose. Paying attention to these intricate elements will bring your character to life!

MEET THE ARTIST

HAIMENG CAO

As a child, Haimeng Cao was heavily influenced by his father's architectural design books. His interest in thinking up striking new cityscapes never faded, and after studying at the renowned ArtCenter College of Design, he has gone on to work as a concept artist on a variety of projects spanning film, games, and a science fiction themed commercial for Walmart. We asked Haimeng about his art, creative journey, and where he finds his inspiration.

Hi Haimeng! Thank you so much for sharing your art with us. For those who are new to your work, please could you tell us a little bit about yourself?

I am a freelance concept artist based in Los Angeles. My family were a big influence on my art when I was a child. My father is an architectural designer, so I grew up with his structure and design books. Those memories and influences still affect the themes in my work and my way of thinking. I love architecture and it's almost become my secondary area of expertise. I read those books when I was young and had many ideas for potential cityscapes. Designing different possibilities of city structures, architecture styles, ecological environments, and social systems in science-fiction worlds is something I'm really passionate about.

Studying at the ArtCenter College of Design was one of the most important experiences of my creative journey. The school is famous for its professional design training, giving me really solid knowledge for when I started work as a concept artist.

Working for different companies and on a variety of themed projects has brought me opportunities to explore more creative fields and a chance to research things I knew little about before. Creating brings me happiness and passion, and I would love to be challenged further in the future.

Your background knowledge of architecture has obviously shaped your work to include fantastical cityscapes, but do you consider yourself as having a "style"? What do you believe inspires your work?

I do not consider myself to have a unique rendering style. However, each series of work has its own style in order to tell the story and convey the mood. Every piece has a unique camera angle and displays spectacular panoramics of the city. Each city has different architecture styles and atmospheres. The story is established within those techniques. I enjoy travelling to different countries when I can; it's an important door to stimulating inspiration. Book-reading and film-watching are my main activities during weekends. I enjoy dystopian novels, and find them visually inspiring.

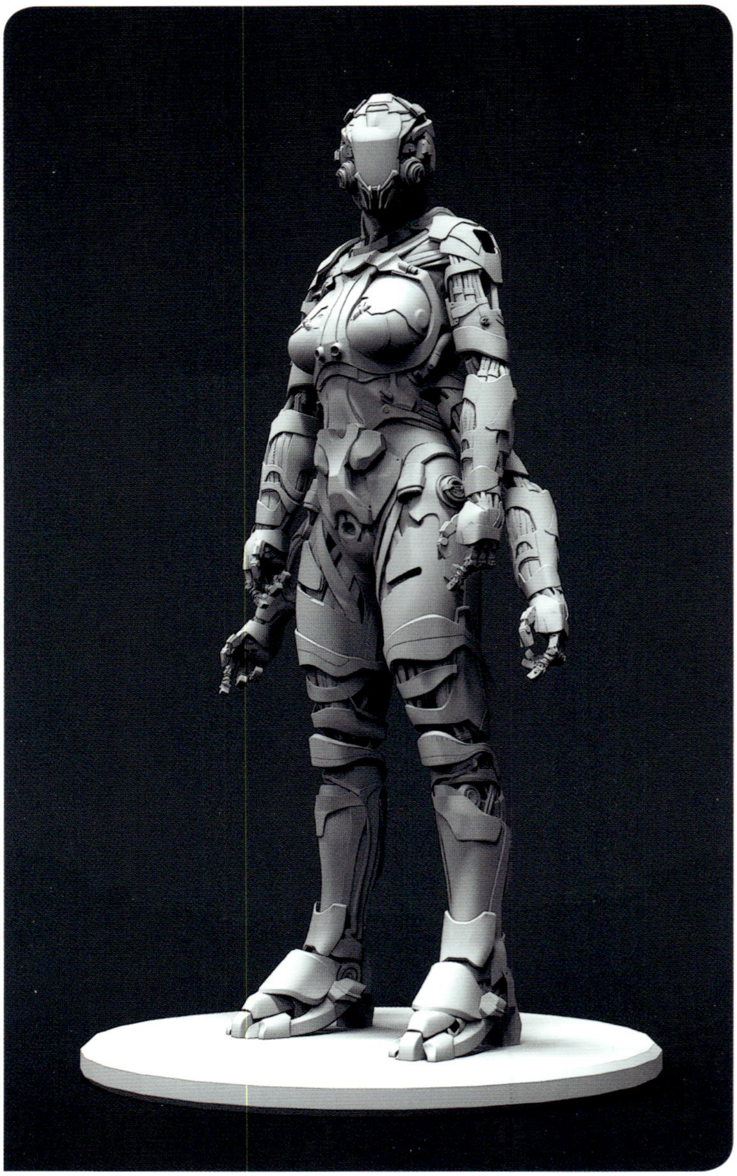

"I ENJOY DYSTOPIAN NOVELS, AND FIND THEM VISUALLY INSPIRING"

This page: *Battle Angel* – A 3D model based on a human-shaped figure

Opposite page (top): Architectural drawing created with marker pens

Opposite page (bottom): *City Rig System* – A rig system is the theme of this piece – architecture and vehicles surround this central structure. Details on the platform emphasize the scale

4006

Where are your favorite places to travel to? Which location has inspired you the most?

Japan is one of my favorite countries to travel to. Church on the Water is one of the places which has inspired me the most. The church is located on the island of Hokkaido in Japan and was designed by the modernist architect Tadao Ando. The building is surrounded by the forest and is reflected in the water, so it works beautifully with the natural environment. The space and mood brought me peace. Those impressions influenced my work a lot and pushed me to think about the abstract elements that artists need to convey with gamers when they journey into the game world.

"COMMUNICATION AND COLLABORATION BETWEEN ARTISTS AND PRODUCERS ARE CRUCIAL FOR PUSHING A PROJECT FORWARD"

You have worked at Blizzard Entertainment and Framestore as well as working for yourself as a freelance artist, how do the experiences compare?

I worked as a concept artist at Blizzard Entertainment, working with the creative director and the lead artist for their upcoming games, as well as undertaking cinematic concept work for the upcoming film *Dune*, directed by Denis Villeneuve.

We had daily meetings and conversations when working together in the office. Communication and collaboration between artists and producers are crucial for pushing a project forward. It's a shame when an attractive piece of artwork does not fit in the world or story of the project. The situation is quite different for a self-employed freelance artist where you may have more freedom and control over the work, and time to push personal work to the next level. Or you may get the opportunity to work on a variety of different projects over a period of time. Currently, I enjoy the freelance work, as it gives me the freedom to be a part of a variety of projects and spend more time with my family.

This spread: Artwork from *Theseus*

"I RELY ON MY IMAGINATION AND REALISTIC PHOTO REFERENCE"

Which projects are your favorite to work on, and why?

The commercial for Walmart, directed by award-winning director Marc Forster, is one of my favorite projects I have worked on. The story is set in a future science-fiction world, which is filled with downfallen cities and low technology robots. Several children find a Walmart receipt, which begins their fantastic journey. We spent several weeks developing the visual direction of the world. Since the commercial was several minutes long, every element in the shot had to have its own impressive territory to convey the background of the world. Our love of the story made us passionate about polishing all of the details. It successfully premiered during the 2017 Oscars.

What did you use for inspiration to design for the Walmart commercial? Do you rely on your imagination when developing science fiction?

The director Marc Forster asked us to look at the work of Swedish artist Simon Stålenhag. His work specializes around the theme of stereotypical Swedish countryside environments and futuristic science-fictional machinery, which was very helpful for the narrative of the Walmart commercial. Personally, I rely on my imagination and realistic photo reference for guidance when creating. I like to visit different locations and take photos, with or without a particular purpose. I love sketching and taking notes at a location for several hours for inspiration, and I regularly study popular science-fiction artwork to grasp current trends in the industry.

This page: Environment linework

Opposite page: Character designs for a recent project

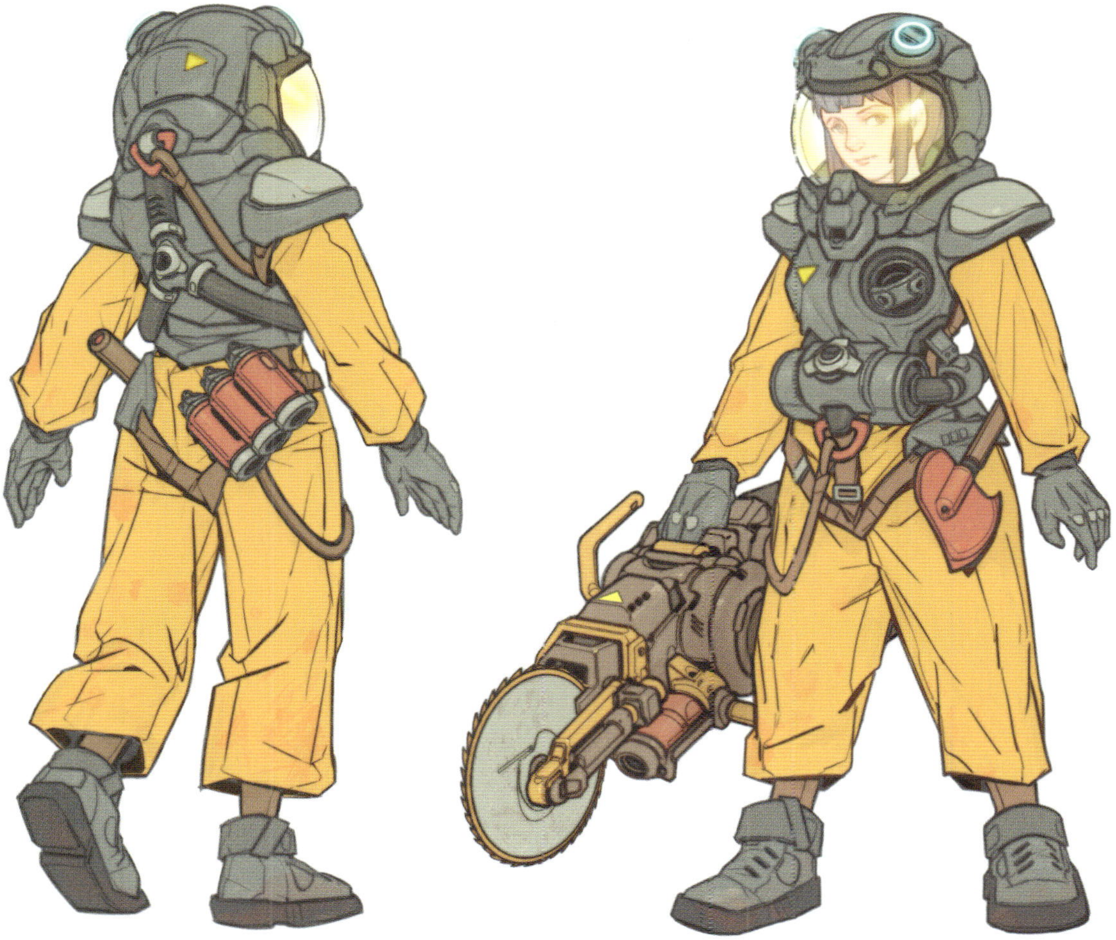

You design a range of different elements for world-building, including creatures, machines, buildings, and characters. How do you approach the character development process and how does it differ to designing creatures or inanimate objects?

The character development is treated as a part of the world-building process, and all elements must have consistency, including architecture, vehicles, and creatures. I push character design and other parts of the world simultaneously.

What kind of environmental and social system does the character live in? How does the background story affect the character's motivation and personality? Is the design of the character based on a particular culture in the real world? I like to ask myself these questions, or talk with the creative director and art director regularly. Once we have those answers, it's easier and quicker for artists to move forward and ensure the design of the character is visually accurate and consistent.

For the design of creatures or robots, I pay more attention to their physical structures. Sophisticated anatomy and spatial organization can make inanimate objects visually interesting. But unlike creatures or robots, character design allows for more direct personality and humanity, which is the most important medium to emotionally communicate and connect with audiences. For animated storytelling especially, the characters should be set at a very early stage.

This page: Linework for *Unmasked Girl* - a story of self-consciousness and identity

What advice can you offer to budding concept artists about how to be noticed by game design studios?

An effective online presence is very important for any new artist, in order to show off their work and welcome new opportunities. The challenge is to keep sharing work regularly and make sure people know they can make contact with you when they have an appropriate project. Balancing time spent between personal work and freelance work will also help to improve and expand your portfolio.

Just remember to keep learning and don't worry if your current major isn't concept design. For example, one of my creative colleagues studied history at university, but his alternative educational background makes his work unique and impressive. The experience gained from different academic disciplines feeds into the final artwork.

Do you have any plans for the future? What would you like to be involved with next?

I would love to join companies outside of the United States, such as in Japan or China. Their projects face different markets and the experience would be helpful in learning industry trends around the world. In the future, I would love to work on a project with interesting narrative storytelling – developing a new world means a beginning of a new and enjoyable journey. I also hope to get involved with more stylized tasks and to train as a more versatile artist.

STORYTELLING THROUGH GESTURE

SAMANTHA VILFORT

I started out like many of us, in middle school homeroom drawing characters straight, with arms behind their backs. It took me years and years to discover that gesture could make those stiff drawings come to life, and even as a story artist I'm still learning! Storytelling through gesture is the best tool in your arsenal to wordlessly communicate the vivid character in your mind. Gesture is the secret sauce that takes your character designs from pretty drawings, to stories that your audience want to know more about. So, where do we start?

WHO ARE THEY?

I want to draw a knight. My natural instinct is to reach for a stock standing pose, but instead I stop myself and consider what kind of person she would be. After an intense battle protecting the innocent, she's in good spirits, maybe even tossing a wink towards an onlooker. The picture of confidence and ease. A nice, long line of action with a follow-through of hair sets her apart from her sterner colleagues. She loves her life.

WHAT DO THEY LIKE?

Who would this knight fall in love with? Maybe a fair lord in a neighboring kingdom who reveals his dreams of romance in the music he creates. When I draw the lord, I pay attention to curling the gesture inward, making the lyre he's holding feel like his most important treasure as he sings his latest love ballad.

"WHEN UPSET, HORSES TURN THEIR EARS BACKWARDS, SO I USED THIS GESTURE TO COMMUNICATE HIS DISPLEASURE"

HOW DO THEY FEEL?

Every knight needs a trusty steed, and our knight's horse is a bit touchier than most. By understanding an animal's unique body language you can depict readable reactions that you may not be able to get across in a human character. For example, when upset, horses turn their ears backwards, so I used this gesture here to communicate his displeasure.

WHAT ARE THEY DOING?

Every charming couple has their enemies, so unfortunately for the knight and her lord, a wild witch has her eyes set on their destruction. In her latest attempt to ruin them, I make the witch's gesture a little awkward. Legs akimbo, arms crooked, she puts all her energy into casting another evil spell and shows that she was clearly never palace-trained.

"THE TRICK IS TO CONSIDER THEIR GESTURES WORKING TOGETHER ON THE PAGE"

HOW DO THEY FEEL ABOUT OTHERS?

Gesture isn't always a solo act; some of my favorite drawings use multiple characters. The trick is to consider their gestures working together on the page. So, for a young couple in love, their bodies use parallel lines of action to make them feel like one gesture, one person, because that's how close they feel as they run into each other's arms.

But maybe they're mortal enemies locked in a battle to the death! The witch and the knight are fighting! With the witch, perched on her rock, I wanted her body language to insinuate she's maybe not quite human anymore, hence the animalistic crouch above her enemy. How is the battle going? Not well for our knight, who sprawls defiantly beneath her. When characters are in love their gestures complement each other, but when they conflict, those gestures have to work against one another.

Regardless of the complexity of your story, gesture is about clarity. It's not about beautiful drawings; it's about presenting character clearly, just as an actor would in a film. Clarity is your top priority! If the hands look strange and the proportions aren't quite where you want them, you've still told your story if people can connect to and understand the drawing.

EAT YOUR DRAWING VEGETABLES!

My favorite drawing activity is going to a figure drawing class and creating a character out of the model's poses by asking myself the same questions I've laid out here. It's low pressure: you never have to show it to anyone, and it pushes my storytelling and drawing muscles simultaneously.

Meet the artist:

KELSEY BUZZELL

Energetic illustrator, Kelsey Buzzell talks to us about her creative expedition from architecture and interior design, to illustration for children's books. Discover how her love for midcentury design drew her into many areas of the design industries and encouraged her bold use of color and subtly geometric form. Take her invaluable advice on board and you will feel more confident navigating and enjoying the world of character design.

All images © Kelsey Buzzell

Hi Kelsey, thank you for taking the time to chat to *CDQ*! To start us off, could you tell us a little bit about yourself and your artwork?

Hi! I am an illustrator and designer living in the Pacific Northwest of America. I work primarily digitally and a lot of my work is brightly colored and quirky: I especially enjoy drawing eccentric human and animal characters and making up back stories for my illustrations. I am always hoping to tell a story with the art I create and to present something whimsical and inviting. My work is typically a combination of digital and traditional media. I enjoy making textures by hand and using them to enhance the final digital work, and I love to experiment with different techniques.

I am formally trained as a designer and I have a Bachelor's degree in Architecture and a Master's in Interior Design, and I rediscovered drawing as a creative outlet from my full-time architecture job several years ago. Illustration became something I would do non-stop in my free time, so I eventually let that inspire me to pursue it as a career. I am currently focusing on illustration for children's books, though I am interested in working in a variety of industries as I continue to grow my craft.

> "... CHILDREN ARE SUCH A GREAT AUDIENCE BECAUSE THEY ARE STILL LEARNING RAPIDLY AND THE WORLD IS WIDE OPEN FOR INTERPRETATION THROUGH THEIR EYES"

Children's book illustrations are a very popular genre among artists; what is it about children's books specifically that attracts you?

I think I was drawn to working in children's books because of the storytelling aspects of the art. I really love books and stories and I think it's amazing to have the opportunity to have a share in making them. It is fun to think about how to represent a story through pictures (sometimes entirely so) and how to make something that isn't in the text read visually, like a fun puzzle.

I also think that children are such a great audience because they are still learning rapidly and the world is wide open for interpretation through their eyes. Getting to make art for children allows you to tap into the naivety of the child-like part of your brain, which means as an artist you get to think about the world through a different lens – and in some ways maybe escape a little bit. I like the idea that I could make something that helps a child dream about a fantastical place or adventure, and I really love how children's book art comes in many different forms and styles – there is such a wide array of published work out there that is endlessly inspiring.

The people I have met in the industry have also been extremely welcoming and friendly, which is another huge bonus when you think about illustration as a career – working with friendly people is always a plus!

This image:
Bloody Mary – A friendly take on the folklore of Blood Mary

Opposite page:
Funky Lady

Your illustrations have a distinctly vintage style – do you think this was inspired by your love for vintage finds?

I think that a lot of my style is based on things I visually consume, as well as things I have always been somewhat drawn to or inspired by. One of those inspirations is definitely vintage design and products. I grew up watching midcentury movies and musicals and I find a particular charm in vintage goods. It is so much more fun to find something at an estate sale or thrift store than it is to shop for something new – you find more unique items in general and it feels like a reward when you find something really cool.

In college, I was also inspired by midcentury architectural designs and furniture. As I started to explore art more seriously, I unconsciously infused a vintage flavor into my style, and every time I come across a "new to me" midcentury illustrator, I get very excited! I remember discovering Mary Blair's body of work several years ago and it really striking me – I felt an instant connection to it. I think the simplicity of color and form, the timelessness of the style, and then the soft handmade textures found in vintage illustrations, has definitely inspired my work.

Opposite page:
Rainy Day Girl

Right: *Crow House*

You mentioned that you "find more unique items in general" when shopping for vintage items – do you have any pieces that you find particularly inspirational to your creative work?

I have a decent sized collection of vintage Pyrex, glassware, and other midcentury home goods – those come in really fun patterns and colors that I find to be inspirational. I have a bunch of them displayed in a midcentury hutch in my kitchen. My favorite find so far though, is an amazing painting of a tiger that I found at an estate sale. It is gorgeous; the colors – greens, yellows, golds, and orange – are super vibrant and it fits in perfectly with our mixed and matched vintage furniture items. It's hard to find good vintage art at estate sales, so when I saw it, I had to have it.

"... THE SIMPLICITY OF COLOR AND FORM, THE TIMELESSNESS OF THE STYLE, AND THEN THE SOFT HANDMADE TEXTURES FOUND IN VINTAGE ILLUSTRATIONS HAS DEFINITELY INSPIRED MY WORK"

This image:
The Dragon and the Lighthouse

Opposite page:
Country Mouse

"THERE IS A FREEDOM AND PLAYFULNESS IN THE WORLD OF ILLUSTRATION, AND IT OPENED UP NEW STORYTELLING POSSIBILITIES FOR ME"

It's so interesting that you previously studied architecture and interior design, yet have become an illustrator. What do you think drew you to illustration? And do you think that your interior design and architecture knowledge informed your style of drawing in any way?

I really loved my education in design and I think this has informed the way I work through problems and approach illustrative designs; I understand concept, idea generation, color schemes, perspective, space, and light pretty well because of my education. I also think it taught me discipline and how to persevere: putting in the hours and hard work comes naturally. That being said, what I really love about illustration is that I get to break some of the rules I was taught existed while in architecture school and in my career as a designer – with illustration I can get messy and communicate the quirky aspects of life and create scenes that exist in an imaginary world.

Buildings don't have to be made with logically placed lines, or be right-side up and people and animals can be giants – anything goes! There is a freedom and playfulness in the world of illustration, and it opened up new storytelling possibilities for me.

What is it about the ability to tell stories through art that is so appealing?

I think the fact that a visual story can be interpreted in different ways is really powerful. Each person who views a piece of art may notice something different or have a different take on how the piece makes them feel. I really love that art can bridge divides and cross communication barriers – you don't need words or text to experience a piece of art or a picture book. Art can be shared and appreciated by a diverse group of people.

In your artist statement you say that you find inspiration from "animals, plants, and minerals, both real and fantastical" – which is your favorite to draw and why?

I love to draw it all, but I enjoy drawing animals the most. First, I am an animal lover through and through, and second, I find animals so fascinating. There are so many of them to discover; I will watch any nature documentary that features animals.

I also think animals have such fun personalities and when you draw them you get to enhance that. They can be given human-like reactions and you can play off their quirky faces and bodies. I have always loved Richard Scarry's books and enjoyed looking at all the different animals doing the things that people do. Animals acting like people inevitably brings joy!

Above: *A Llama Playing the Bango*

Left: *An Iguana Playing the Fiddle*

Opposite page (top): *Blackbird Holiday Hubub*

Opposite page (bottom): *A Donkey Playing the Bells* – All three creatures were ceated for an Inktober challenge

"ANIMALS ACTING LIKE PEOPLE INEVITABLY BRINGS JOY!"

Which animal is your favorite to draw and why?

I would typically probably say anything cute and furry, but if you look at my portfolio, I have one animal that shows up more than others... and that is a crow or raven. I have always really liked crows and find them to be really interesting animals. They are super smart, can learn tricks, remember faces, and have their own personalities and rituals. They also traditionally get a bad rap and are associated with magic and omens, and thus have a kind of edginess to them; making them really fun to draw as a mischievous character type, which I particularly love drawing. Also, fun side note: one of my cats is named Crow!

"I LIKE MIXING BRIGHT COLORS AND QUIRKY CHARACTERS WITHIN A SLIGHTLY EDGIER, AND SOMETIMES SPOOKIER, CONTEXT"

This page: *Graveyard Girl*

Opposite page: *Nova* – Nova and her giant mountain crow, Obi, are the bringers of night; slowly turning the world to shadows and stars

Although often colorful, and child-friendly, some of your designs have an eerie and slightly unnerving vibe. Is this a conscious decision to reflect your love of horror and mysteries?

Absolutely. I was one of those kids who loved ghost stories and the darker kids movies. I remember checking out books about ghosts and other scary stories from the library and I loved watching scary movies at sleepovers. I also grew up watching mysteries on television and the opening sequence for *MYSTERY!*, drawn by Edward Gorey, was one of my favorite things to catch before bed. I love folktales, Sherlock Holmes, and Agatha Christie. I am drawn to the "unknown" and themes that weave themselves through horror stories and mysteries. So, it is something I aim to achieve, but I also think it comes out naturally.

I don't want everything I make to be eerie or unnerving, but with some of my pieces I want to give a nod to my former kid-self. I think there is a place for scarier or spooky things in children-focused illustration work. So, where appropriate, I like mixing bright colors and quirky characters within a slightly edgier, and sometimes spookier, context.

You mention that you like to incorporate handmade textures into your digital work – what exactly do you mean? And why do you choose to do this?

I love traditional media and a lot of the artists I have been inspired by (both past and present) either use traditional media or create digitally in a way that has more of a handmade feel. There is something I really like about how you can create a little more depth and softness by using paints or pencils and layering techniques.

That being said, I work much more quickly digitally and love the flexibility that digital tools provide. You can fix things when you mess up without having to paint over it and color correct in layers with a click! So, to get the look I am drawn to, but also use the tools that work best for me, I have created some workflows that allow me to bring handmade textures into my pieces. This typically involves me using paint, ink, or pencils to make textures on paper, which I then scan and use as overlays on my images. Sometimes I use one, sometimes I use a few, and I plan to keep experimenting.

What I have found is that these textures and their natural imperfections can't be replicated digitally, so it is better to make them by hand and then bring them into the digital work than try to figure out a way to make them digitally. I also try to use digital brushes that complement the handmade textures (gouache brushes with a slight opacity and chunky pencil effects are my favorites right now). Occasionally, I scan in pencil lines and digitally paint over them, which also helps provide a looseness to the work that isn't there when using digital pencils.

Finally, do you have any advice to readers with no previous creative experience, but are considering getting into illustration?

Draw a lot and put in the time to make it a priority. Do your research and have an idea of what kind of work you'd like to do and what the steps are to move forward in those avenues. I spent a lot of time gathering information early on in my illustration career. I woke up early just so I could draw before work for a while because I knew it would improve my skills, and that I would be less motivated later in the day after work. It was actually really nice waking up early, making coffee and drawing in the quiet of the early morning.

Don't be afraid to share your work – we all grow and improve over long periods of time and just because you aren't happy with your work now doesn't mean it won't get better – most of the artists I know are constantly searching for ways to grow their work and hone their voice. If you are too scared to share or try something new, you are holding yourself back. Don't compare yourself to others or copy. You will have more success trying to find a unique style and voice.

It is important to take inspiration from other artists, just don't start telling yourself you need to be the "next" version of that artist. Be you, but embrace change.

"DRAW A LOT AND PUT IN THE TIME TO MAKE IT A PRIORITY"

Opposite page: *Hare Shapeshifter*

This page: *Kasa-Obake* – Inspired by Japanese folklore

GALLERY

In every issue we hope to inspire you with superb character designs and character-based artwork from a selection of talented professional artists. This issue features work by:
Helen Bucher | Janice Sung | Marie Gräbener

HELEN BUCHER IS A GRAPHIC DESIGNER PASSIONATE ABOUT CREATING AND DESIGNING CONTENT. SHE LOVES TO EXPRESS HERSELF THROUGH PHOTOGRAPHY, ILLUSTRATION, AND DESIGN. HER VISUAL DEVELOPMENT IS HIGHLY INSPIRED BY FASHION, JAPANESE POP-CULTURE, AND EVERYTHING CUTE.

Helen Bucher | helenbucher.ch |

JANICE IS AN ILLUSTRATOR AND DESIGNER BASED IN TORONTO, CANADA. SHE HAS A PASSION FOR CREATING BEAUTIFUL IMAGERY, OFTEN REVOLVED AROUND FASHION AND BEAUTY. SHE TAKES INSPIRATION FROM THE POSTMODERN MOVEMENT, GRAPHIC DESIGN, ABSTRACT PAINTINGS, AND BEAUTIFUL PHOTOGRAPHS. SHE ENJOYS COMBINING ORGANIC FORMS WITH INORGANIC FORMS TO CREATE AN INTERESTING VISUAL CONTRAST AND AN OVERALL FEEL OF SOPHISTICATION AND SULTRINESS.

Janice Sung | janicesung.com | All images © Janice Sung
JANICESUNG

MARIE GRÄBENER IS AN ILLUSTRATOR AND COMIC BOOK AUTHOR FROM GERMANY. HER PASSION IS TELLING STORIES AND CREATING WORLDS FULL OF ADVENTURES UNDER HER PSEUDONYM KRAKEN ILLUSTRATIONS. HER ARTISTIC INFLUENCES INCLUDE NOELLE STEVENSON, HEIKALA, AND RUMIKO TAKAHASHI.

Kraken Illustrations | instagram.com/kraken_illustrations | All images © Marie Gräbener

HOW TO KEEP A SKETCHBOOK

JOSE CICERARO

Keeping a sketchbook is one of my all-time favorite things. On any given day I have about four sketchbooks on me – I would be lost without them!

In this tutorial I'm going to share some insight into how I keep and manage a sketchbook, the tools I use, as well as some techniques and mindsets to try while you're sketching. Remember, sketchbooks are a place for you to explore and have fun, as well as create a backlog of future project ideas and prompts.

START AS YOU MEAN TO GO ON

This was the first page in a new sketchbook. I decided to test out the paper quality by drawing one of my original characters. I knew there wasn't going to be another sketch on the left-hand page, so decided to continue some of the elements onto it. I also wanted to add a little mystery to the sketch by including sinister silhouetted characters jumping out. Elements like this also act as memos when I'm taking it to completion. These little reminders can go a long way, demonstrating the importance of showing your work and getting your ideas down on the page.

"THE VARIETY OF DIFFERENT LINE WEIGHTS YOU CAN GET FROM ONE BRUSH IS REALLY IMPRESSIVE"

BREAK THE FRAME

Here's another first page. Again, there's something really satisfying about breaking the frame. The paper in this watercolor sketchbook is seriously smooth, making it perfect for inking. My goal here was to ink this goblin, concentrating on line quality and contrast. I also wanted to retain the life and energy of the sketch. Using a brush pen is great. Not only are they portable, but the variety of different line weights you can get from one brush is really impressive. Sketchbooks are perfect for this type of exploration.

HEADS OR TAILS

I love using interesting aspect ratios. The square format of the Illo sketchbook makes it one of my favorite books to sketch in. It has loads of awesome features and great paper too. I kept rendering and exploring different textures with this spread, playing with light intensity while trying out a variety of shapes and styles. It's important to try new things and to document your experimentation on page. Sketching with a goal in mind can be really beneficial to your growth as an artist, but it's also incredibly liberating to have a stress-free space to try stuff out too.

MONKEY AROUND

In this sketch I was focusing on using bold graphic shapes. I used a Copic N0 marker for the underdrawing, and once that was dry, I refined the drawing with a Pentel 0.7mm mechanical pencil filled with blue lead. Another focus of this sketch was the linework. I wanted bold lines to contrast with the texture of the hair and achieved this look by outlining the stroke and bringing it to a point. Drawing on a smooth watercolor sketchbook allowed for a nice build-up of value with the waxy blue lead. Sometimes the paper makes all the difference.

BRUSH PEN SILHOUETTES

I really enjoy using a brush pen for silhouette exploration. I use a medium tip and love the coverage this enables you to achieve. It's nice to change-up how you use your tools. Most of the pieces I ink have a more traditional thick line, but I love the energy a brush pen can lend to silhouettes. It also fills the form easily and adds great texture.
If you want to add something extra to your silhouettes, try using a white marker.

Thinking in terms of shape and negative space will help you get to the core of an idea and accentuate the focal points. This technique is a great way to warm up or cool down.

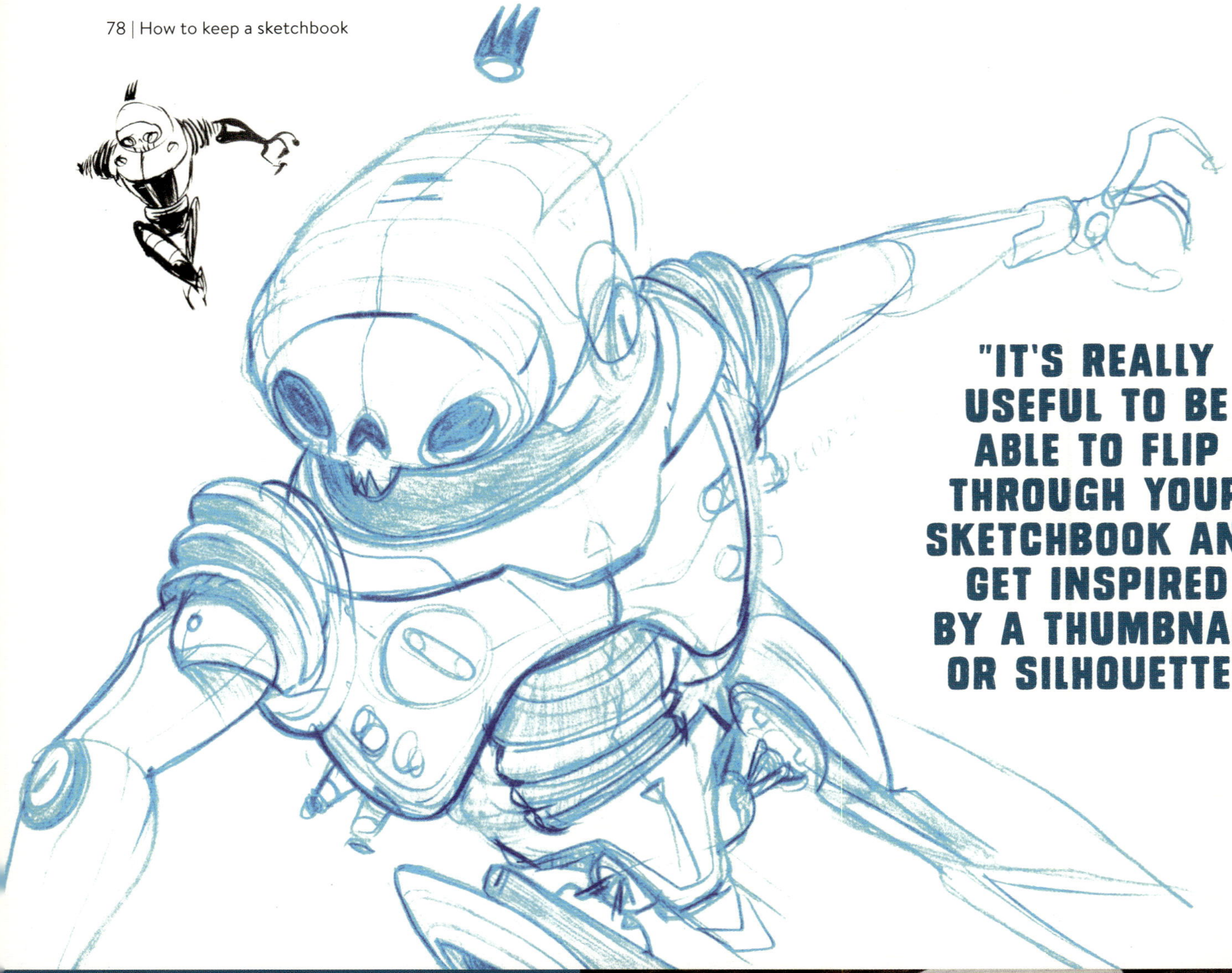

"IT'S REALLY USEFUL TO BE ABLE TO FLIP THROUGH YOUR SKETCHBOOK AND GET INSPIRED BY A THUMBNAIL OR SILHOUETTE"

SKULLBOT DEVELOPMENT

Inspired by the silhouettes on the previous page, I wanted to explore this character a little more. I really liked the boxy head, hand and leg shapes from the thumbnail. Some details changed, but that's to be expected. Building libraries of idea prompts is a great thing to use your sketchbook for. It's really useful to be able to flip through your sketchbook and get inspired by a thumbnail or silhouette. Getting ideas out and onto the paper frees up space in your head to generate more ideas. Try and dedicate time to sketching every day.

CONSTRUCTING ROBOTS

Robots were the focus on this page. Here, I wanted to explore different robot shapes and attributes, experimenting with layers and plates, and trying to imagine how things would actually be built. I often flip back through my sketchbooks when I need ideas – every page and every character has potential. One of the many benefits of a sketchbook is the freedom to experiment and explore. When it feels right, I like to add some extra value to my sketches. All of those little touches add up and can make a sketch feel more finished. Using wax pencils is a great way to build up layers.

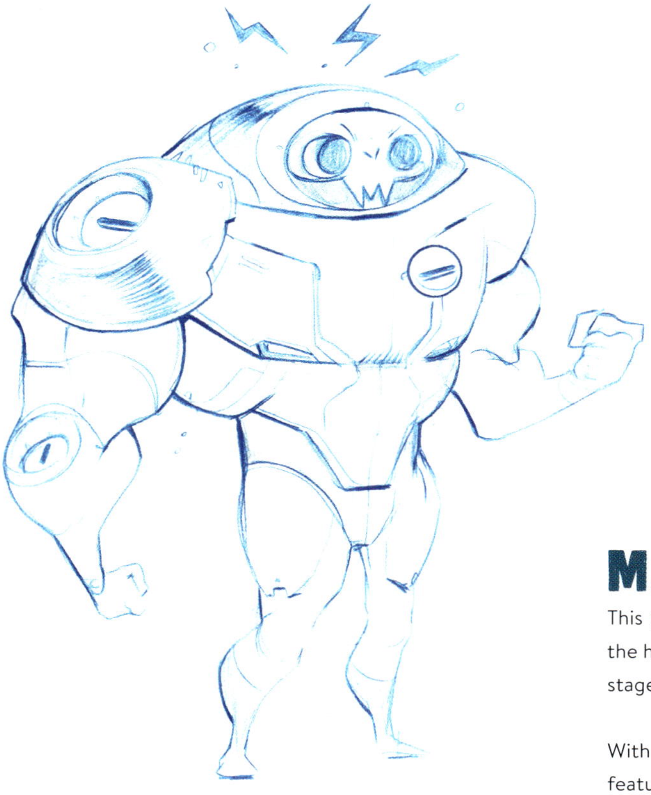

MAKING ADJUSTMENTS

This page started with a marker underdrawing. I blocked out the rough shapes for the heads and figure. I knew I wanted to draw a robot type character and in the early stages decided that I wanted to put a skull in the dome.

With the other drawings I wanted to push and pull some shapes; to create exaggerated features, such as long chins and stubby noses. I really like how simply adjusting the spacing of some of the features can give your character a totally new look and feel.

EXPLORING SHAPES

This page was all about exploring character types with rounded features. Aside from the character in the middle, using rounded shapes is a great way to make non-villainous characters. Using a wax color pencil allows you to hold it sideways and get some great value. Plus, using wax pencils in you sketchbook also keeps things from smudging. I love designing heads and exploring as many character types as possible this way.

MIGHTY TEAMS

I'm a big fan of teams in stories. I like to explore different types of characters and picture them working together in a group. I've really taken to the shapes used for the central pig character. I love the bell-shaped head and large features. Adding props offers a fun way to ground your drawings and give them a little more life. I love pushing shapes and as a result tend to draw a lot of large noses. An example of this is the co-pilot in the upper right corner. A sketchbook is a great place to get ideas out and try new techniques.

"JUST BECAUSE IT'S A SKETCHBOOK, DOESN'T MEAN YOU CAN'T BE PRECISE"

PRECISION DOODLING

I had 80s cartoons and space pirates on the brain with this one. I started how I usually do, with a marker underdrawing, then continued with a pencil pass. I was working on clustering details and pushing shapes – contrasting straight lines against curves can add a lot to a drawing. I love the contrast of those types of lines. Having the rough marker underdrawing made it easy to figure out the rest of the robots' details. Don't forget to use templates or rulers if you have them. Just because it's a sketchbook, doesn't mean you can't be precise.

PENSIVE PIRATES

Shapes and pirates were the focus of this page. I wanted to explore a variety of broad shapes, playing around with different combinations, including eye shapes. I like the contrast between a circular eye socket and an oval pupil, and vice versa. It's also good to consider the balance between complexity and simplicity. Before you start, it can be helpful to come up with a motif to focus a sketch on. Sometimes all you need is a word prompt to get the ideas flowing. Why not try writing a different word on a few pages of your sketchbook, then designing characters based on that word.

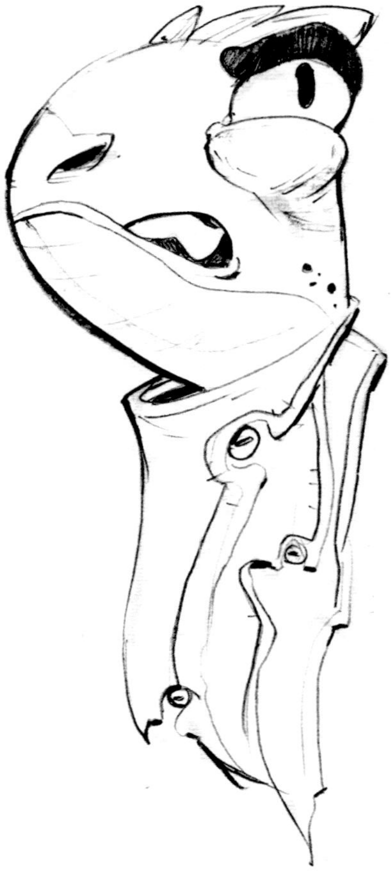

GOBLIN CRAFTING

I love the fantasy genre and especially love drawing goblins. I love the shapes, the silhouettes, and the big ears! Here I focused on traditional traits – big ears and nose – while trying to vary the spacing to keep things interesting. I love to cluster areas of interest and make shapes a little longer or shorter than I'm initially comfortable with. Having the marker underdrawing as a guide is really helpful, as it allows you to work past it and step out of your comfort zone a bit. With the type of stylization and characters I love to sketch, crazy proportions are a must.

"I LOVE THE FANTASY GENRE AND ESPECIALLY LOVE DRAWING GOBLINS"

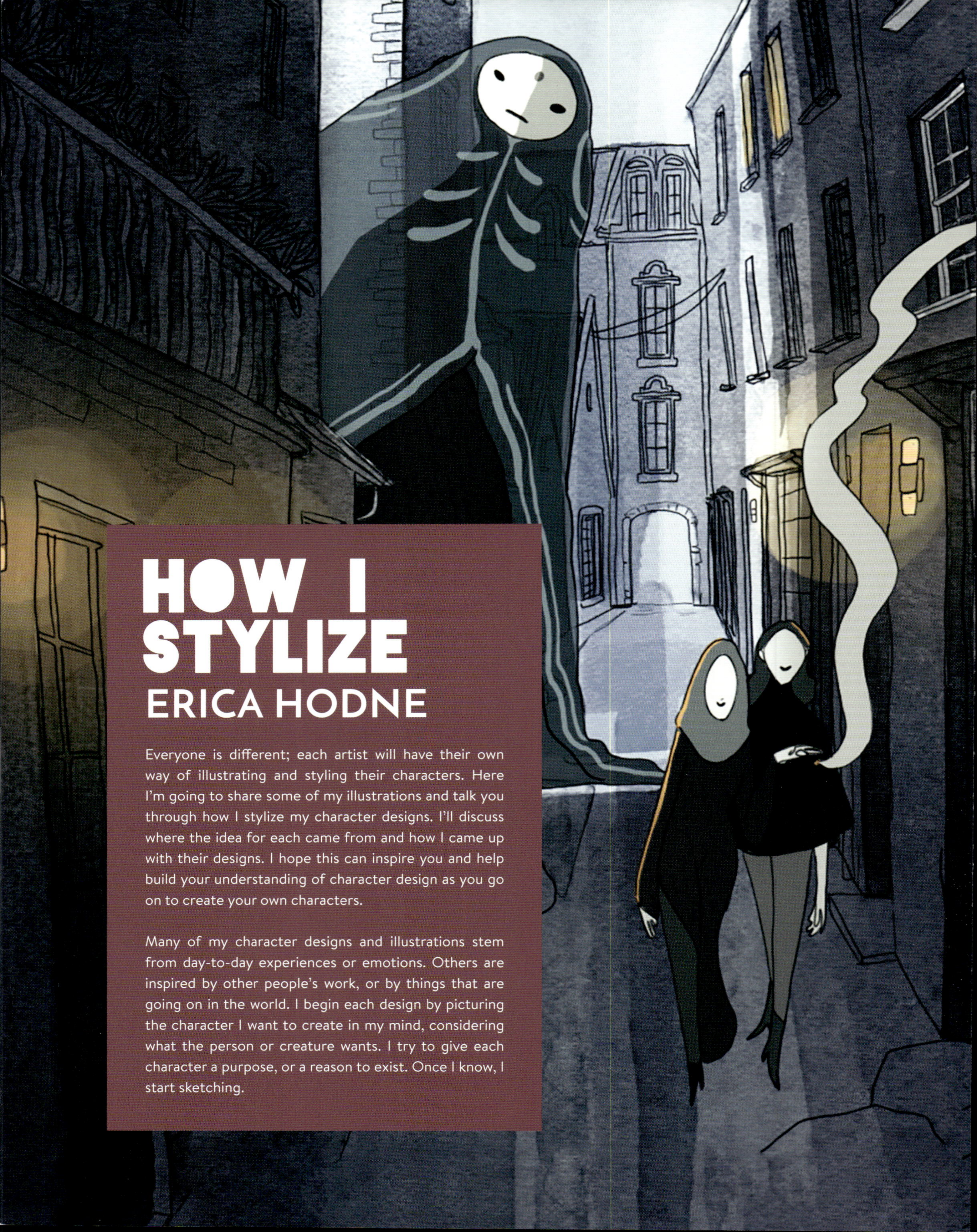

HOW I STYLIZE

ERICA HODNE

Everyone is different; each artist will have their own way of illustrating and styling their characters. Here I'm going to share some of my illustrations and talk you through how I stylize my character designs. I'll discuss where the idea for each came from and how I came up with their designs. I hope this can inspire you and help build your understanding of character design as you go on to create your own characters.

Many of my character designs and illustrations stem from day-to-day experiences or emotions. Others are inspired by other people's work, or by things that are going on in the world. I begin each design by picturing the character I want to create in my mind, considering what the person or creature wants. I try to give each character a purpose, or a reason to exist. Once I know, I start sketching.

DRAW WHAT YOU KNOW

Here we have *The Panna Cotta Lady*. I created her for the Character Design Challenge on Facebook when the theme was "Candy People". It's always a challenge to come up with an original idea for the CDC and I admit I struggled with this one. But a great technique I've learned over the years is, when you hit an artistic block or struggle to think of something to draw, just draw what you know. In this case, I'd eaten my first panna cotta dessert the night before, which gave me the idea to draw this little lady.

FEELINGS AND EMOTIONS

I used a similar technique when coming up with this lettuce child sketch, which I called *All Grown Up*. I wanted to use a character to communicate how it feels to supposedly be all grown up, but still feel like you're half stuck in the ground. I took inspiration from pretty pictures of lettuces and kale on Instagram, combining them with this emotion to create the lettuce child.

FEARS AND THE UNNERVING

This spooky portrait is a piece I produced for the Character Design Challenge when the theme was ghosts. I took inspiration from my fear of old portraits. I was unnerved to find out that in the past, portraits were sometimes taken of, and with, the recently deceased. Now, whenever I see these kinds of family portraits, I always picture a ghost standing in the background.

COLLABORATION AND STIMULUS

Here are two designs I produced for a project I worked on with some friends where we set out to depict the nature spirits of London. I was very inspired by Hayao Miyazaki's work when I designed these characters. I wanted them to look gray and tired from all the pollution they have to endure, but to still have those spots and lines of light to remind them of what they once were.

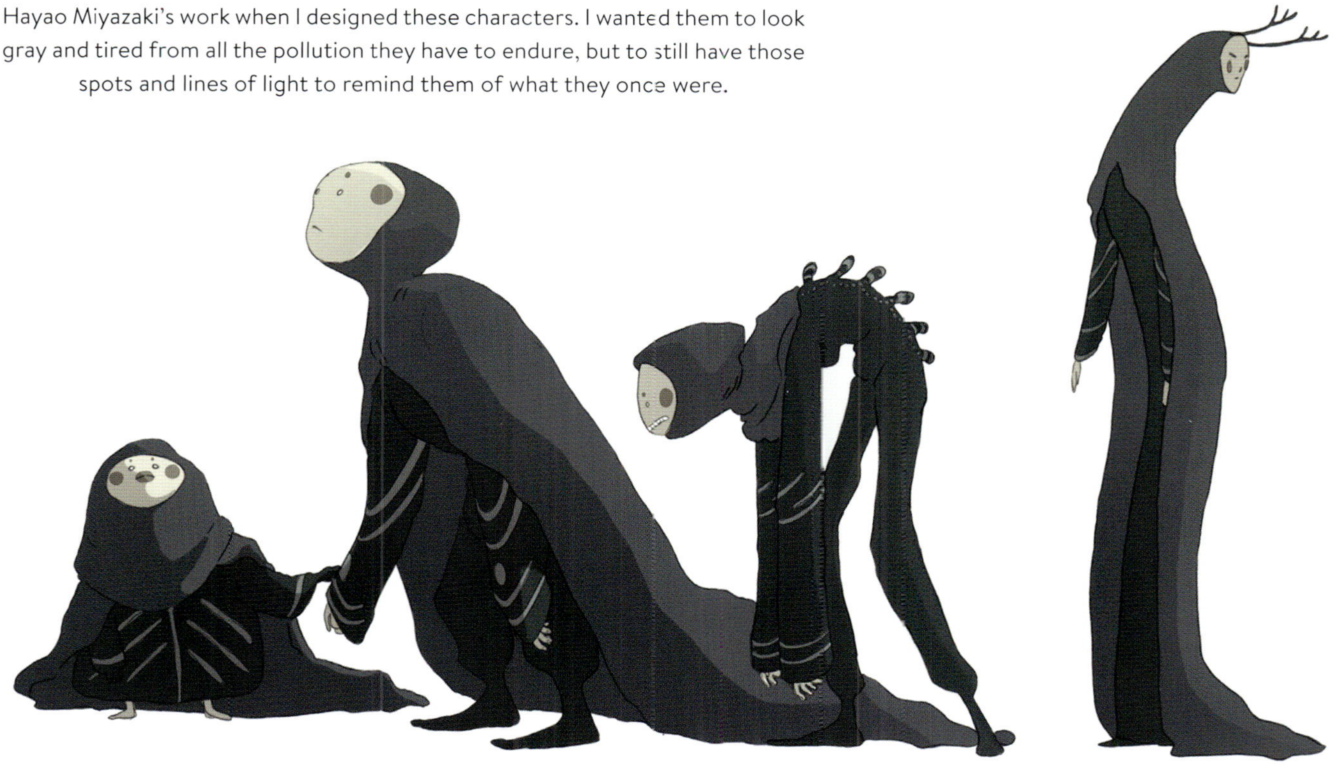

COLOR AND MOOD

This is a character I am currently working on for a short film that will be out soon. *Melankoli* is a film about mental health, exploring the emotions a person might feel and situations they may find themselves in when experiencing sadness and depression. I used a gray, washed out color palette to reflect the character's low mood. I also gave her long, unkempt hair, as she does not have the energy and mental strength to take care of it. I wanted her to almost look sick, but like a sick person trying to appear healthy. Remember, every aspect of your character means something.

HUMANOID VS. MAGICAL

The above illustration is called *Should We Eat It?* These characters have been with me for a while; I first started thinking about them back in 2010. I wanted them to be humanoid animals, but also somewhat magical. I envision them being able to give other living beings the same value as we humans each give ourselves.

DRAW, DRAW, THEN DRAW SOME MORE...

If you want to break into the industry, I suggest you draw a lot, and draw a variety of different things, to build up a strong portfolio.

REDESIGNING CLASSIC CHARACTERS: EVIL QUEEN

IOANA SOPOV

We're all very familiar with character tropes such as the evil queen. They're present in fairy tales, animation, literature, comic books, and movies. But what if we could take these classic character tropes and reinterpret them? In this tutorial we're going to do just that – study what this type of character represents and how it's portrayed in media, then find a way to breathe new life into the design and concept. We'll kick things off by doing some serious research and then use fundamental character design principles such as shape language and line of action to create our own updated version of an evil queen.

DO YOUR RESEARCH

Any character design assignment, especially when relating to a design refresh, should start with a fair bit of research. You should look into existing designs and try to find not only what they have in common, but also what sets each one apart. Think about design, but also take into account the personality and motive of each of these characters. Try expanding your research area to other cultures and mediums, such as theatre, or comic books, to get fresh insight. Why is this character so common throughout stories? What does it symbolize on a deeper level?

WHAT TO KEEP

Decide what common themes of the character you want to keep or reverse. You can either try a completely opposite approach to the classic one, creating a character that looks the opposite of an evil queen, but secretly is one. Or, just reverse one or two things, creating contrast. For example, instead of a plotting, magical queen, why not make her into a fearsome warrior? Go from question to question until you have a solid grasp on who your character is. Go back to your initial research to get inspiration for backstory themes and questions to ask. Your answers will help flesh out your character's personality and design.

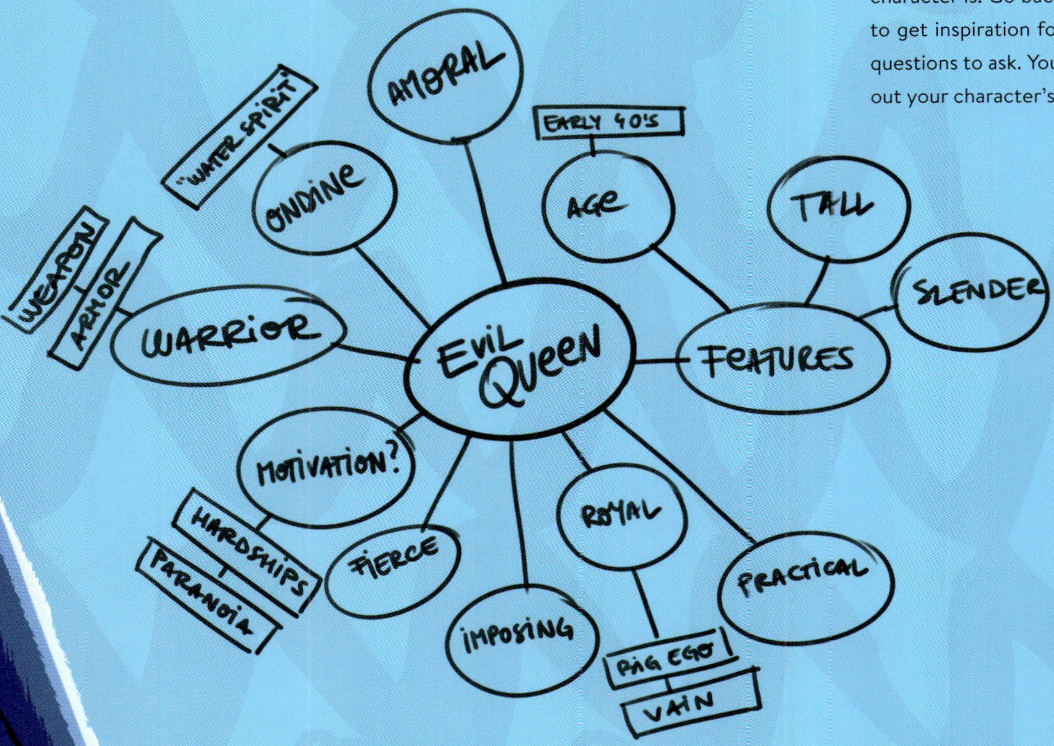

Above: Collate references and study the silhouettes of existing designs

Left: Draw a simple mind map of possible traits

IDEAS

- Replace classic dress/robes with:
  - A) Armor & cape
  - B) An androginous costume
- Understated crown
- Less makeup, maybe more like war paint?
- Brighter accent colors in costume
- Long, flowing hair
- Replace high, sharp collar with imposing shoulder pieces

IDEAS

- Hide/obscure face with collar
- Angular shoulder pieces to balance thin frame
- Big hair/completely obscured by hair
- Sharp angles in dress cut

ROUGH IDEAS FOR REFRESH

This is when you start writing down rough ideas for the design, taking into account the general themes you've researched, your new character's backstory and personality, and potential design ideas derived from existing designs. Think about what elements you would like to keep from existing stereotypes and what you will change and why. Laying out some rough design silhouettes or thumbnails at this stage will help you with generating ideas. Don't worry about creating beautiful drawings; just use black and maybe a couple of gray values to quickly explore silhouette concepts.

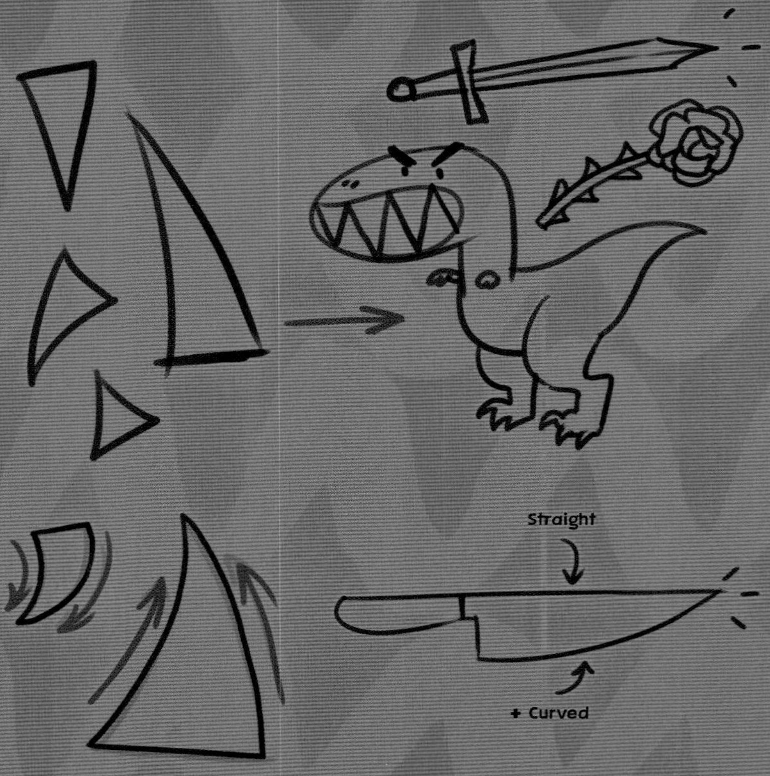

STRAIGHT OR CURVED?

As the character is an antagonist, or anti-hero at best, and we've decided to make her into a warrior-type queen, we want the shapes we use in her design to reflect that. Sharper lines and angles remind us of teeth, spikes and other pointy things, and suggest more dangerous, aggressive traits. While we want to incorporate these traits into our design explorations, that doesn't mean ignoring curvy lines completely. The sharpness of a shape is often emphasized by contrasting curves, for example in the design of a butcher's knife.

THUMBNAILING

After doing the research and generating some rough ideas to start with, it's time to let loose and start drawing. Thumbnails are small, rough drawings meant to give you freedom to explore ideas without committing too much time. Focus on shape language, negative space, and proportions. Avoid detail and keep things simple by just using a couple of values. While existing designs are rather rounded or bulky, we're looking for a sleek, sharp figure, perhaps balanced out by a cape or something similar.

Opposite page (top): Play around with possible design ideas, using silhouettes to help

Opposite page (bottom): Sharp and curved shapes and what themes/traits they convey

This page: Quick thumbnails with simple values and shape language emphasis

THUMBNAILING MANIA

Try different approaches toward drawing thumbnails: lay out large blobby shapes and draw what you see in them; scribble using one continuous line; look for interesting silhouettes in the objects around you – bottles, lamps, whatever you find draws your attention; play around with shape proportions, regardless of anatomy.

"LOOK FOR INTERESTING SILHOUETTES IN THE OBJECTS AROUND YOU – BOTTLES, LAMPS, WHATEVER YOU FIND DRAWS YOUR ATTENTION"

REFINE THUMBNAILS

This is where you can pick two or three thumbnails that you like, and believe fit your vision best, then develop them further. Turn down the Opacity on your thumbnails and sketch out what your character could look like on top. At this stage you might realize that some proportions need adjustments or more exaggeration, so this is a good time to experiment and either push things further or rein them in.

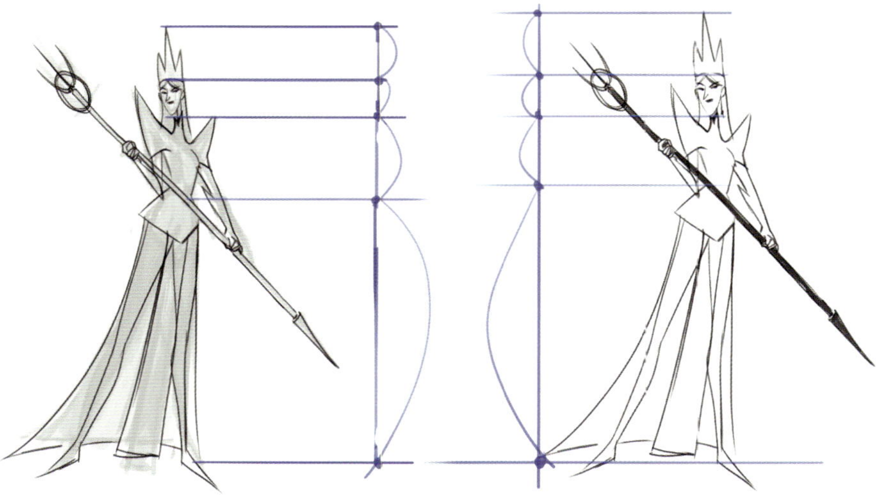

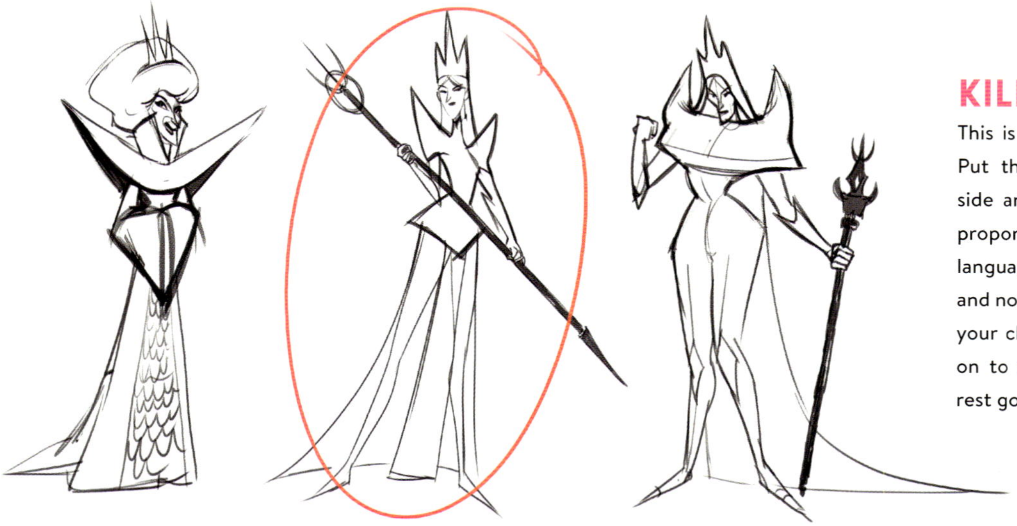

KILLING IDEAS

This is where you'll have to make a choice. Put the resulting rough sketches side-by-side and compare them. Look for the best proportions, lines of action, and shape language. Look back at your initial research and notes and figure out which one best suits your chosen character traits. That one goes on to the next stage of development. The rest go into the ideas trash can.

"EXPLORE THE CHARACTER'S BODY LANGUAGE AND HOW THE DESIGN IS AFFECTED BY DIFFERENT POSES"

POSING EXPLORATION

After establishing what sketch you're going to focus on, the next step is to explore the character's body language and how the design is affected by different poses. This is a good opportunity to find out what works in the design and what doesn't, as well as which poses best illustrate your character's personality. It's also a good exercise to help you figure out some other aspects of the design you might not have considered until now. For example, how the outfit reacts to movement or seated positions.

Opposite page (top): Draw on top of thumbnails while adjusting and pushing proportions and refining design

Opposite page (bottom): Evaluate sketches and choose one design to move forward with

This page: Try out different poses

STRIKING A POSE

Pick a pose to present your character in. The line of action of the pose, often the center line of the character, gives the impression of movement to the drawing. The shoulder and hip axes also accentuate the dynamism of the pose. At this stage it's important to focus on how expressive the pose is, so using the line of action and axes of the pose, push for as much dynamism as you can while also taking into account the balance of the character. This is a good opportunity to refine the shape language as well.

VOLUME

Even though you're working in a 2D space, a good character design has volume and three-dimensionality. You should map out the volume and shape of your character before adding details. Imagine that your character is covered in a wireframe and the lines indicate not only volume, but perspective too. When you think of the volumes of your character's design, it will be easier to render it in such a way that it translates as a fully 3D form to the viewer, even if you only render it in linework.

"PROPORTIONS ARE KEY, SO AS YOU BEGIN SKETCHING, EXPERIMENT WITH DIFFERENT SIZES FOR THE MAIN THIRDS IN WHICH YOU CAN SPLIT A FACE"

FACIAL CONSTRUCTION

When starting to design the face, you should always look back to your notes. A lot of your character's personality is going to shine through their features and expression. Proportions are key, so as you begin sketching, experiment with different sizes for the main thirds in which you can split a face: forehead, eyes and nose, as well as mouth and chin. A common design trait of current evil queen characters is very arched, thin eyebrows with heavy eyeshadow. Perhaps find a different way to express femininity, but also a bit of danger, by lowering the brows towards the eyes, giving the character a more mysterious look.

Opposite page (top): Push the initial pose for more expressive appeal

Opposite page (bottom): Figure out the volumes and shapes of the design

This page: Sketch different proportions and features

"INSERTING LITTLE ASYMMETRIES INTO OUR CHARACTER'S EXPRESSIONS WILL MAKE THEM LOOK MORE BELIEVABLE AND ALIVE"

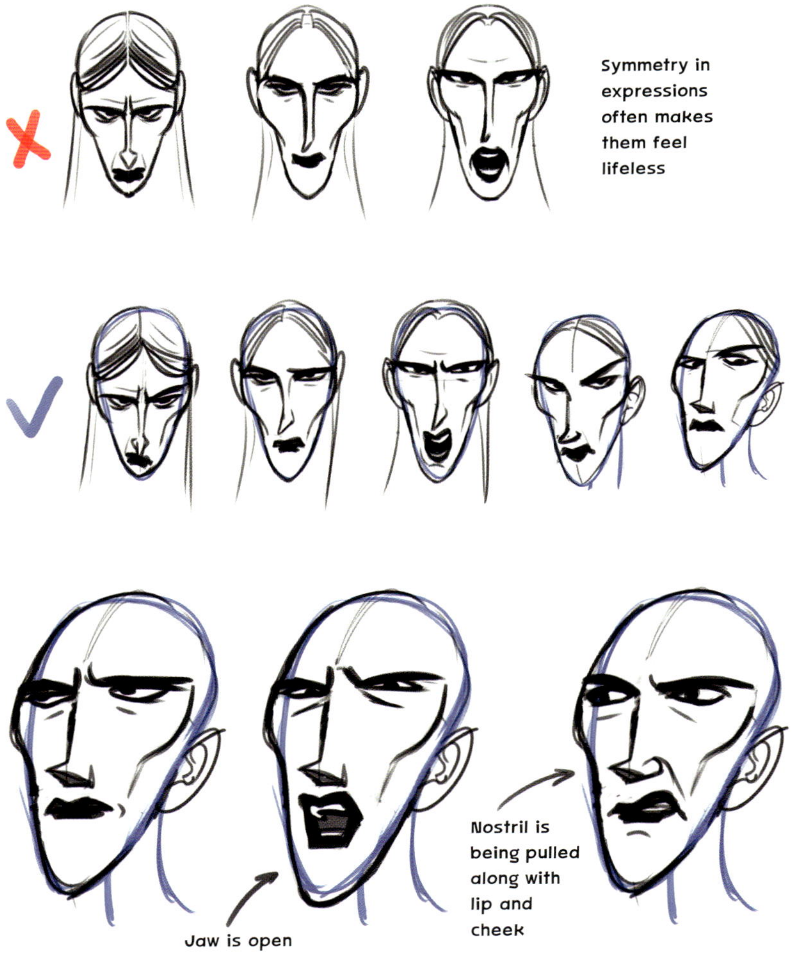

ENGAGING EXPRESSIONS

Starting from the base head shape and proportions, try out different expressions and emotions on your character's face. Photo references are always helpful. If not, take a couple of selfies acting out the expression you want to draw using your phone or camera. Try to avoid symmetry in the facial features, as it can often make expressions appear lifeless and boring. Add a small wrinkle on one side. Lift one eyebrow a bit higher. Open one eye more than the other. No one's face is symmetrical in real life, so inserting little asymmetries into our character's expressions will make them look more believable and alive.

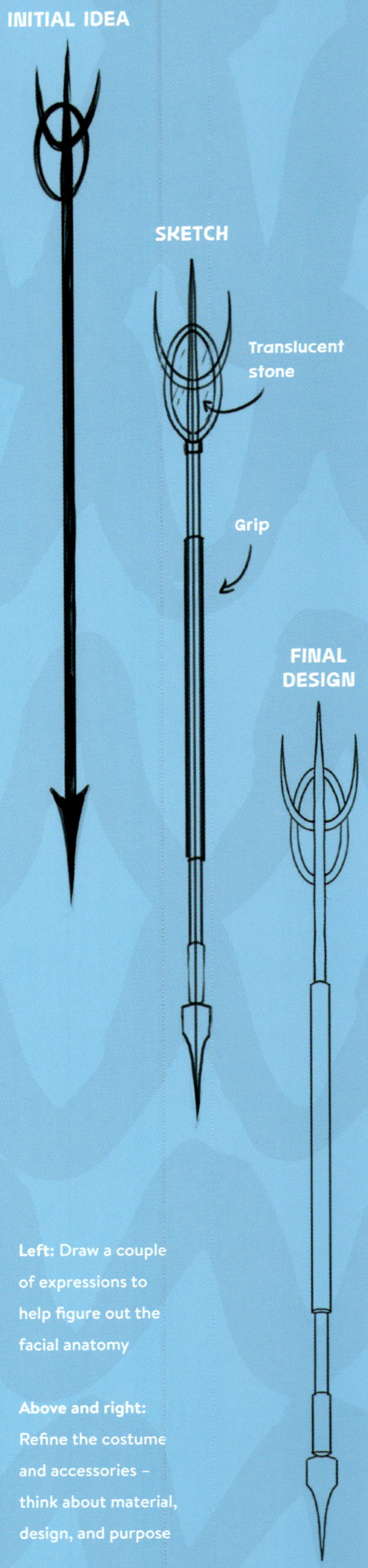

Left: Draw a couple of expressions to help figure out the facial anatomy

Above and right: Refine the costume and accessories – think about material, design, and purpose

DRESS TO IMPRESS

Think about the backstory of your character. This evil queen comes from the Land of the Seven Lakes and is named Ondine – a type of water spirit. Look for textures and elements that connect with your character's personality and origin to add to the outfit design. This is where references will be your friend. Also think practically; what role does each piece of her outfit tell you about her life and attitude? In the original design trope, the sceptre is usually a symbol of power or an accessory to the character's dubious magic powers. Consider what other uses a sceptre could have... It could also be used as a weapon, so why not incorporate new design elements from that area?

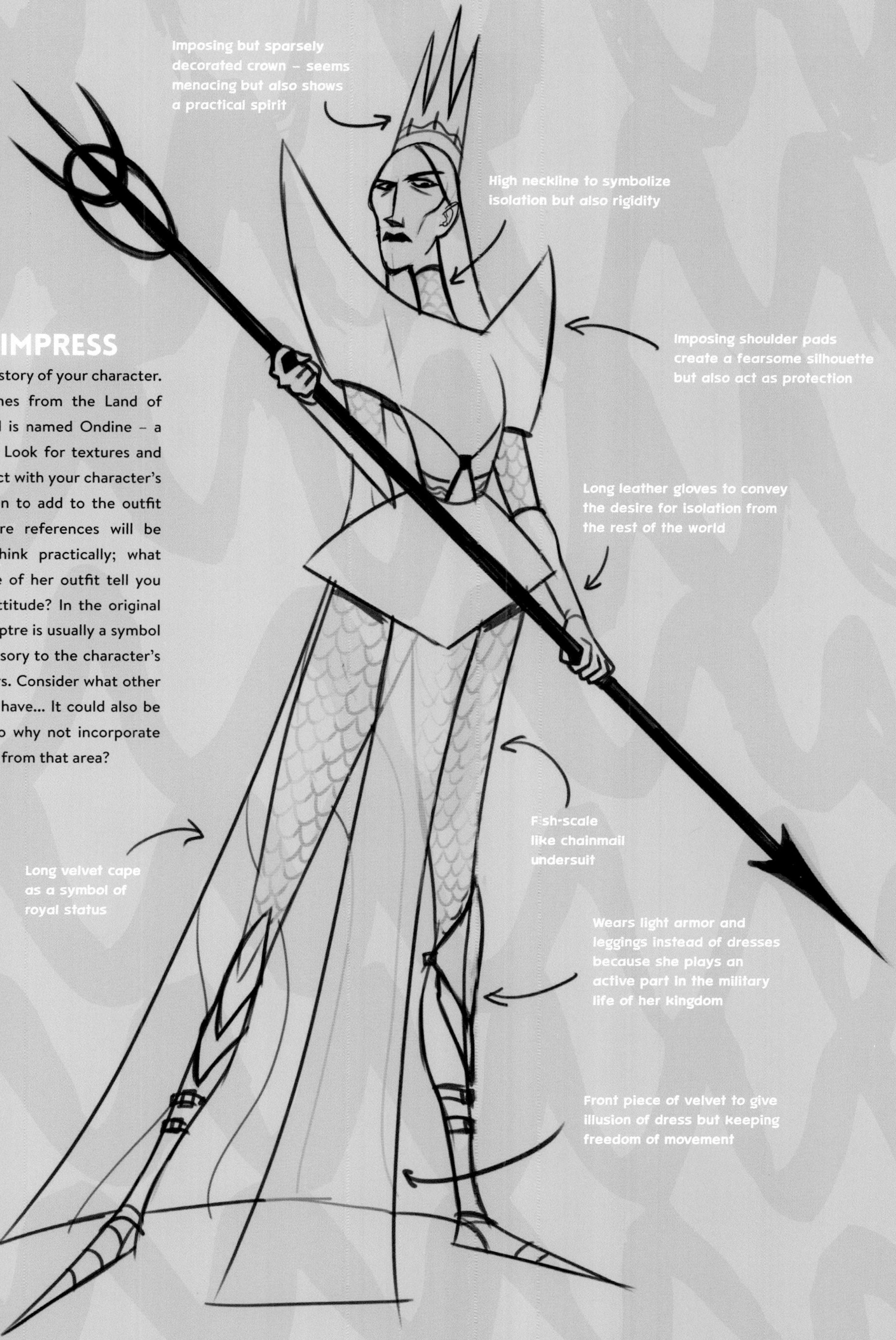

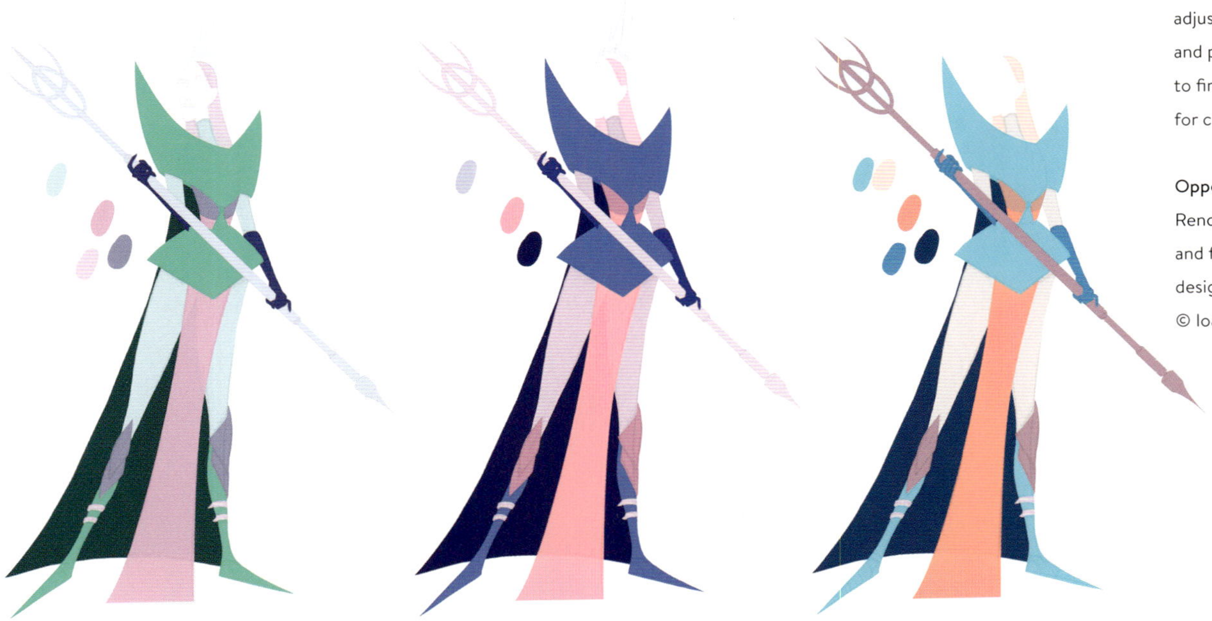

This page: Use adjustment layers and paint overs to find options for colors

Opposite page: Render, add details and finish up the design. Final image © Ioana Sopov

BRAVE COLOR CHOICES

When refreshing an existing design trope, sometimes changing one essential component is enough to give it a new lease of life. In this case, existing designs focus almost exclusively on dark palettes with accents of red or purple. Going against the grain, you can experiment with different types of colors, safe in the knowledge that the design already indicates the fearsome nature of our evil queen. Lower the sketch Opacity to 5-10% and start adding your colors underneath. Try to keep elements and different materials on different layers when doing so. This will come in super handy when trying out different color combinations using adjustment layers, for example.

FINALIZE YOUR DESIGN

Whatever style you decide to use for rendering, the last step is all about texture and lighting. Here you also have the opportunity to figure out other details, such as the type of materials used in the outfit as well as whether you want to add a backdrop that supports the character.

It's important to know when to stop with rendering and let the design speak for itself. Use adjustment layers freely to correct tone and contrast until you're happy with the desired result. Even if you work directly in color, it's always a good idea to check your values in black and white. A good design should have enough contrast and variation between the values.

CONTRIBUTORS

TOM BOOTH

Author/Illustrator and
Art Director
instagram.com/tomwilltell

Art director and production artist, Tom is a critically acclaimed author of children's books, including *Don't Blink!* and *This Is Christmas*.

KELSEY BUZZELL

Freelance Illustrator
kelseybuzzell.com

Kelsey is an Oregon-based designer with a background in architecture and interior design focusing on children's book illustration.

HAIMENG CAO

Concept Artist
artstation.com/haimengcao

Haimeng works on visual development and concept design, with a particular focus on science-fiction cityscapes.

JOSE CICERARO

Senior UI Artist at
Insomniac Games
instagram.com/superspaceocto

Lover of cartoons and comics, Jose works at Insomniac Games by day and by night he is an illustrator and graphic designer.

FEDERICO ETCHEGARAY

Storyboard Artist at
DreamEast Pictures
fedetch.com

Federico moved to the USA from Uruguay to study animation. He has worked for Studio Yotta, DreamEast Pictures, and Disney TV.

ERICA HODNE

Animator at Tiger Aspect
instagram.com/eeurekaa

Erica is an animator, illustrator, and storyteller working for Tiger Aspect in London as an animator on the *Mr. Bean* animated series.

ISAAC JADRAQUE

Digital Artist
instagram.com/jadgoo

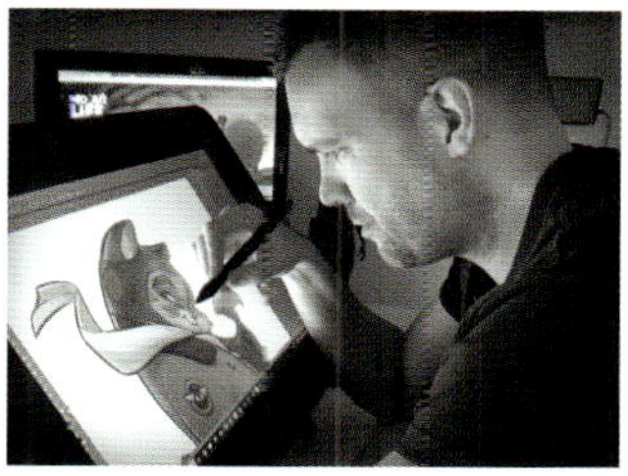

Isaac specializes in character design, utilizing UX/UI design skills in his work on animation, films, children's series, and advertising.

CORAH LOUISE

Freelance Illustrator and
Character Designer
corahlouise.com

Corah is a freelance illustrator and character designer with a passion for telling stories through quirky colors and designs.

IOANA ŞOPOV

Freelance Illustrator and Animator
ioanasopov.com

Ioana is an illustrator and animator based in Bucharest. A huge fangirl, she loves experimenting with different styles and techniques.

SAMANTHA VILFORT

Story Artist at Walt Disney
Animation Studios
samanthavilfort.com

Since graduating in 2017, Samantha has experienced a whirlwind of creativity while working at Walt Disney Animation Studios.